ST. LOUIS'
BEER CULTURE

BREW
IN THE
LOU

PAST, PRESENT
& FUTURE

ST. LOUIS POST-DISPATCH
BOOKS

ST. LOUIS'
BEER CULTURE

BREW
IN THE
LOU

PAST, PRESENT
& FUTURE

BY EVAN S. BENN
ST. LOUIS POST-DISPATCH HIP HOPS COLUMNIST

ST. LOUIS POST-DISPATCH
BOOKS

BREW IN THE LOU

ST. LOUIS' BEER CULTURE – PAST, PRESENT AND FUTURE

BY EVAN S. BENN

ART, PHOTO & DESIGN EDITING
WADE WILSON

COPY EDITING
JODY MITORI
MIKE SMITH

CONTRIBUTING WRITER
JEFF HERMAN

SALES & MARKETING
ANGIE CLARK
CORY PAROLIN

Special thanks to Doug Weaver of Kansas City Star Books

Softcover
ISBN 978-0-9842084-6-3

Printed by Walsworth Publishing Co., Marceline, Mo.

To order additional copies, call **1-877-POSTSTL** (1-877-767-8785)

Order online at **www.thepost-dispatchstore.com**

CONTENTS

| INTRO | # BEER IS IN THE AIR |

BEER HELPED WRITE ST. LOUIS' HISTORY

When I moved to St. Louis in 2009, the first thing I did after unpacking was order a pint of Budweiser from a bar near my downtown loft. When in Rome, right? I remember thinking how that beer, served alongside a pulled-pork sandwich, tasted remarkably fresh. And it's no wonder: I was sitting less than two miles from the prolific brewery where my beer was made.

The very next morning, I stepped outside to walk to my new job at the St. Louis Post-Dispatch, and I smelled something that stopped me in my tracks. I deeply inhaled, taking in that heady aroma that almost smells like someone roasting damp breakfast cereal in an oven. It was, of course, beer being brewed at Anheuser-Busch InBev's St. Louis flagship – aka "The Brewery."

It was at that moment that I started to understand how integral beer is to the fabric of this city. For more than 150 years, the business of beer has provided jobs to St. Louisans, and the consumption of it has been part of our family gatherings, sporting events and nights out with friends. Beer helped write St. Louis' history, and today a new generation of local breweries is poised to shape the area's future.

The St. Louis Post-Dispatch has long recognized the important relationship between St. Louis and beer. The P-D is committed to covering beer from both business and lifestyle perspectives. While the paper's Business desk does an admirable job of keeping tabs on the beer industry, especially as it pertains to A-B InBev, I get to handle the fun part – telling the stories of the hardworking brewers who make beer and the happy consumers who imbibe it.

The A-B takeover by InBev was still fresh on people's minds when I got to town. But a new story line quickly began to unfold here: the rise of craft beer.

The craft-beer movement dates to the early 1980s, soon after the federal government lifted restrictions on homebrewing. Pre-eminent beer writer Michael Jackson had piqued a newfound interest with his "The World Guide to Beer," and pioneering breweries like Anchor (Anchor Steam), Sierra Nevada (Sierra Nevada Pale Ale) and Boston Beer Co. (Samuel Adams Boston Lager) started to open eyes and taste buds to the flavors and possibilities of craft beer.

HIP HOPS WITH EVAN BENN

Tom Schlafly and Dan Kopman put St. Louis on the craft-beer map when they opened the Schlafly Tap Room – home to St. Louis Brewery – downtown in 1991. Theirs was the first new brewery in St. Louis since Prohibition, the federal edict that lasted from 1920-1933 and pushed most of the city's breweries into bankruptcy.

In 2011, as Schlafly Beer celebrates its 20th year in business, craft-beer's boom in St. Louis has reached a new high. From Cape Girardeau to Ferguson, almost 20 craft breweries and brewpubs dot the landscape, with new ones opening with increasing frequency. Out-of-state craft breweries have identified St. Louis as a beer-loving market, and they've been tripping over each other to get their beers in our refrigerators and into our bar taps. And local restaurateurs – who long ignored craft beer in favor of wine or Budweiser – have begun to see the value, both economic and culinary, in offering smartly edited lists of fresh and seasonal beers.

St. Louis is riding a craft-beer wave, and we don't appear to be getting off any time soon. To keep readers up to date with the latest craft-beer news, reviews and events – and to help separate the swill from the sublime – the P-D tapped me to oversee Hip Hops, our print column and daily blog devoted to all things related to beer in St. Louis. I expanded Hip Hops to Twitter and Facebook, because I wanted to have the immediate communication and interaction with the craft-beer community that social-media sites provide. And the P-D recently launched a Hip Hops app to bring all of these elements – news, reviews, blog posts, tweets and more – together in one place, available for free at your fingertips.

"Brew in the Lou" is meant to be a collection and continuation of that work – the stories of the brewers, breweries and beer enthusiasts in St. Louis – rather than a comprehensive history of brewing here. My goal: To tell the tale of beer's past, present and future in the Gateway City, with an eye toward how we got to where we are today, and where we're going tomorrow. What you'll find is a collection of stories, photographs, fact boxes and more about beer in St. Louis, from the earliest days of lagering caves to the recent explosion of craft breweries and brewpubs.

My dive into the world of craft beer has been refreshing, invigorating, enlightening – and delicious. People craftier than I have found ways to combine four simple ingredients – water, malted barley, yeast and hops – into dozens of styles of a magical beverage. My respect for beer, and the professionals and homebrewers who make it, comes from the complex balance of art and science – not to mention patience and constant cleaning – required to brew a perfect batch. Drinking it up has become more than a job for me; it's a hobby, a lifestyle, an obsession. But, if you'll believe it, what I like more so than drinking beer is listening to people talk about it. Hearing craft-beer enthusiasts – particularly those in St. Louis – spout their passions for their favorite breweries, styles, hops, grains and more is more entertaining than any debate between foodies, sports fans or political junkies.

Beer continues to evolve, as do the tastes of its biggest fans. I may want a hoppy India pale ale today, a hearty stout tomorrow. You may have tried a Michelob Shock Top last weekend and decide you'll spend this weekend exploring other Belgian-style witbiers from local craft breweries. You probably know somebody who is a Bud Light man – always has been, always will be, ain't gonna change. And that's fine. What matters most is that St. Louisans continue to responsibly enjoy and appreciate good beer. Only then can we go from being a city with a rich brewing history to a world-class beer destination.

I hope you'll raise a glass of your favorite beverage while reading this book. If you're lucky enough to be doing so in St. Louis, with a St. Louis-made beer, you'll have the added pleasure of knowing that your beer is probably super fresh. And, if you want, you can open a window and take a deep breath. If the wind's blowing the right way, there's a good chance the air will smell like beer being brewed.

Evan S. Benn
St. Louis
May 2011

WANT THE FREE HIP HOPS APP?

Point your smartphone browser to
http://stltoday.com/beerapp

Or read the QR code below.

PAST

Drinkers in a St. Louis speakeasy toast the anticipated end of Prohibition in late 1932. The legal return of low-alcohol beer came on April 7, 1933.

CHAPTER 1 · PAGE 12

THE BEER CAVES

St. Louis' earliest beer pioneers took advantage of the city's natural caves.

CHAPTER 2 · PAGE 22

ON THE MAP

Thanks to Anheuser-Busch, St. Louis and beer will be forever linked.

CHAPTER 3 · PAGE 30

SCHLAFLY BEER

The local craft-beer revolution started at a small downtown brewpub in 1991.

BY EVAN S. BENN

Robin Dieckmann, a handler for the Budweiser Clydesdales,
exercises horses at the Anheuser-Busch Stables located
at One Busch Place in St. Louis.

CHAPTER 1 | # THE BEER CAVES

A BEER CITY FROM THE GROUND UP

Hundreds of years before the first St. Louis beer was brewed, the city had already begun to take shape as a beer town, but it had happened out of sight.

An intricate, random web of caves snaked beneath St. Louis, formed from the erosion of underground limestone deposits. These natural caves, with their cool temperatures, were a boon to early local brewers, who used them for beer storage before commercial refrigeration.

About three dozen breweries called St. Louis home by the mid 1800s, and many of them produced lagers, the type of beer favored by the city's sizable German immigrant population. Lagers, from the German word for storage, require time to ferment at colder temperatures than their sudsy counterparts, ales. The caves of St. Louis offered the perfect lagering environment for local brewers to keep their beers.

Adam Lemp helped introduce German-style lagers to St. Louis. His Western Brewery, founded in 1840, also was among the first to use the city's caves to store its beer. Lemp's son eventually expanded and renamed the business, and the William J. Lemp Brewing Co. became St. Louis' biggest player in the national beer market by the end of the 19th century. One of its biggest rivals was Anheuser-Busch, whose brewery also was built on top of caves.

The Lemp family mansion, which in recent years has operated as a restaurant and inn, is said to be one of the most haunted places in America, thanks to ghosts from Lemps who died in the house. But before the ghosts were (allegedly) there, the family built a series of underground tunnels to connect the area beneath the mansion to the sprawling Lemp Brewery complex nearby. The Lemp family used the tunnels to get to work.

> In 1878, Lemp Brewery produced about 100,000 barrels of beer. In 2010, St. Louis Brewery made about 35,000 barrels of Schlafly beer.

BY EVAN S. BENN

The Lemp mansion, which served as the family's residence and later the brewery's offices, is said to be one of the most haunted places in America. Three members of the Lemp family committed suicide there.

The Lemps and other brewers took advantage of the caves for purposes beyond beer storage (especially once artificial refrigeration became more widely utilized toward the end of the century). The vast area beneath the Lemp complex included a swimming pool – filled with water piped in from the brewery – ballroom, bowling alley and theater. Others ran subterranean saloons and beer gardens. Brothers Franz and Ignatz Uhrig hosted concerts, parties and tours in the caves beneath their brewery near where Union Station stands today.

Prohibition dealt a striking blow to St. Louis' bustling beer industry in the early 1900s. It knocked out Lemp Brewery, but not before the company had the chance to develop a brand it named Falstaff, after a portly Shakespearean character.

Federal agents toss contraband beer bottles into the Mississippi River near Clinton Street in April 1925. Throughout Prohibition, booze kept flowing into the city through trains, trucks and steamboats.

Prohibition lasted 13 years, 10 months, 19 days, 17 hours, 32.5 minutes.

Joseph "Papa Joe" Griesedieck bought the Falstaff rights from the Lemps, and soon he started Falstaff Corp. The company scraped its way through Prohibition by selling soda, de-alcoholized near-beer, and smoked bacon and ham. After the repeal in 1933, Griesedieck's newly renamed Falstaff Brewing Corp. received the first federal brewing permit and got to work right away at churning out pools of beer.

While Falstaff was thriving post-Prohibition, so was another St. Louis brewery, Griesedieck Bros., run by Papa Joe's five nephews. GB beer – called "Slippery Richard" by its fans – grew to great popularity in St. Louis, including a run as the official beer of St. Louis Cardinals radio broadcasts with Harry Caray.

BY EVAN S. BENN

Joseph "Papa Joe" Griesedieck, right, smiles as he receives Federal Permit No. 1 from government agent Louis Becker in 1933. With Prohibition behind him, Griesedieck immediately began brewing pools of his Falstaff Brewing Corp. beer.

It takes only four ingredients to make beer: Malted barley, water, yeast and hops.

Falstaff Brewing Co. bought Griesedieck Bros. from its cousins in 1957 and continued to grow in brewing capacity and distribution scope, peaking at more than 7 million barrels in 1966. But sales began to slide, and in the '70s Falstaff was forced to shut down its breweries – including its original Plant No. 1 in St. Louis – and sell out to the company that produced Pabst beer. Pabst announced in 2005 it was killing off the Falstaff brand.

A Falstaff worker packs bottles of beer into a wooden box bearing the brewery's iconic shield-shaped logo in 1933.

As for other early breweries, Griesedieck Bros. has begun to resurface in recent years. Raymond A. Griesedieck, son of Henry A. Griesedieck, the last president of Griesedieck Bros. before its sale to Falstaff, took control of the old brand in 2010. Its signature German-style pilsner is brewed under contract in Wisconsin, but it is distributed to more than 100 bars, restaurants and liquor stores throughout St. Louis and southern Illinois.

But until the rise of craft beer that St. Louis Brewery ushered in with its Schlafly beer in 1991, one brewery in particular became synonymous with St. Louis. In fact, St. Louisans didn't even need to say the name to know they meant Anheuser-Busch. It's always been, simply, "The Brewery."

America's Oldest Brewery: German immigrant David G. Yuengling founded his brewery in Pottsville, Pa., in 1829. It remains the oldest active brewery in the United States.

BY EVAN S. BENN

BREWERIANA:
THE ART OF BEER-CAN COLLECTING

One person's discarded beer can is another collector's treasure

A display of old beer cans inside the Crown Valley Brewing and Distilling Co.

The first beer can was introduced more than 75 years ago – in January 1935 – by the Krueger Brewing Co. in New Jersey. It marked a revolution in packaging – cans were nearly unbreakable, stacked easily, chilled quickly. And they were colorful.

That last one is key to why Donald Roussin of Maryland Heights, Mo., has more than 8,500 cans displayed in his house. "A lot of them I remember where I got them or from whom. They all have good remembrances," he says.

With 10,000 brewery collectibles – cans, neon signs, bottles, glass and a whole lot more – displayed, beer is represented everywhere in Roussin's home. He even bought the house because its 18-foot cathedral ceilings offered more display space and the reinforced beams let him safely hang his heavier beer signs.

For Roussin, a buyer for Boeing, it all started with beer cans. "It was a fun hobby in high school, and it didn't cost a lot of money. Cans could be found on streets or you could dig them out of trash cans."

Roussin is a member of the Brewery Collectibles Club of America (bcca.com). Founded in St. Louis as the Beer Can Collectors of America, the club has expanded to include other breweriana, much like Roussin's collection.

With so many beer cans produced over the years, and only so much room in basements and houses, a lot of hard-core beer can collectors have taken to focusing their collections.

Take Jed Conroy, an electrical contractor in Bethalto, Ill., who collects cans that have numbers in their name, such as 905, Cloud Nine, 5 Star, Brew 66 and Straight 8 beers.

"I've hit that wall now where it's hard to find numbered cans that aren't so rare they cost a fortune," he said.

His rarest can is a white A-1 Beer test can from Phoenix, and there are only three known to exist. You can see it at beerbythenumbers.com.

By Evan S. Benn

Donald Roussin sits among the more than 8,500 beer cans displayed in his Maryland Heights, Mo., home. Roussin has been collecting cans for more than 30 years.

Others now specialize in number beer cans, but Conroy said, "I'm the original."

Bob Chapman of St. Louis County remembers getting a call at 11:35 one night from another collector who thought he had a can he might want. When he brought over the can and Chapman saw that it was a black St. Louis ABC Old English Ale can, "it took me five seconds to say yes," he recalls, pointing to the can, one of only five known to still exist in this country.

The Lever Bros. retiree once had 20,194 cans but now specializes in Missouri collectibles and cans, including Muehlbach, Country Club, Fishbach and Capital beers. He's partial to items from Griesedieck Bros. in St. Louis and M.K. Goetz Brewing Co. in St. Joseph, Mo., partly because so many people in St. Louis are focused on Anheuser-Busch memorabilia, he explains.

Of his collection, he says, "It's history."

Collinsville, Ill., collector Kevin Kious has focused on Southern Illinois brews and breweries.

On a tour of his collection, he pointed to Highland, Bluff City (Alton) and Mound City (New Athens) memorabilia and noted that East St. Louis was home to the Central Brewing Co., while Belleville breweries turned out Stag, Oldtimer and Stern Brau. There were also breweries in Granite City, Bethalto, Trenton and even Collinsville.

Kevin Kious

"Any town that had 100 Germans in the 1860s had a brewery," says Kious. Kious, Roussin and Henry Herbst, who died in 2009, are the authors of "St. Louis Brews: 200 Years of Brewing in St. Louis, 1809-2009" (Reedy Press, $39.95).

Mike Bender, a head chef at the Veterans Affairs hospitals in St. Louis, specializes in flat-top and cone-top beer cans, and his collection of about 4,000 cans "is pretty much in the basement with some trays lining the walls of the stairs."

The beer can collection complicated his and his wife's search for a home. Bender says he knew they wanted to find a house in Fenton, Mo., when they married in 1983. "Karen and I saw a lot of nice houses, but they wouldn't fit my beer cans."

His wife doesn't mind all of his beer cans. "She collects Precious Moments statues," he says.

Al Kell's specialty is 16-ounce aluminum bottle cans, the newest craze in collecting.

He originally heard Anheuser-Busch was only going to turn out 20 of the "cabottles."

"Heck, I only built shelves for that many," he says. "In no way did I think A-B would put out as many as they did."

The Florissant, Mo., collector, a foreman at a machine shop, now has all 130 of the aluminum bottle cans A-B has produced, and more on the way.

The most unique A-B cabottles are black light cans that appear silver in daylight with the beer label visible only in black light.

Jim Galvin of Belleville, Ill., looks for Storz beer cans at one of the booths at the Gateway chapter of Beer Can Collectors of America show at the Gateway Center in Collinsville, Ill., in 2005.

Can collecting was in its heyday in the '70s and '80s when grade school and high school students were big collectors. Now the BCCA's Gateway Chapter has more than 150 members, and many say the club is as much about the friendships and camaraderie as it is about collecting and trading.

Gerry Schwarz, half of a beer can and breweriana collecting couple in St. Louis County, says, "The BCCA is the best thing that's ever happened to us."

Herb and Gerry Schwarz started collecting in mid-1973 and now have beer collectibles in every room except one bathroom. Lemp and Falstaff plates grace the walls of the dining room and hallway, a restored Lemp St. Louis wood clock hangs in the kitchen, and more than 1,200 cans line a wall in the basement. The two retired civil service employees' basement also includes glasses, beer bottle openers and aluminum bottle cans.

Where will all the beer cans and breweriana of collectors go years from now?

Roussin, whose home resembles a beer can and brewery collectibles museum, says there are plans for a museum in St. Louis. The Brewery Museum Foundation (brewerymuseum.com) is seeking funding for the museum.

CHAPTER 2 # ON THE MAP

ANHEUSER-BUSCH, ST. LOUIS, MISSOURI

"The Brewery," as Anheuser-Busch has been known here since the 19th century, conjures images of many things: Budweiser bottles, towering Clydesdales, the red-brick campus at Broadway and Pestalozzi Street, to name a few.

Even after the company's 2008 takeover by InBev, a Belgian-Brazilian conglomerate, its presence in and around St. Louis continues to be felt.

Hundreds of thousands of visitors each year take tours of the megabrewery here – complete with free samples afterward – and get up-close with the magnificent Clydesdales at Grant's Farm. Locals cheer on their beloved Cardinals at Busch Stadium. University students learn inside brewery-endowed classrooms. And young couples tie the knot at Bevo Mill, a whimsical windmill and now a privately owned event space that August A. Busch Sr. had built in 1916 at Gravois and Morgan Ford roads.

But perhaps what will forever link the brewery to this city, both in the minds of St. Louisans and people around the globe, is the familiar tagline: "Anheuser-Busch, St. Louis, Missouri." For years, we heard it at the end of every Budweiser and Bud Light television and radio commercial and saw it on every brewery logo and advertisement.

After he took control of the company in 1975, August A. Busch III expanded the number of beers A-B produced and beefed up its annual marketing budget to the hundreds of millions of dollars. Soon, the brewery's ad campaigns – some clever, funny or downright silly – became a pop-culture staple, broadcast directly into our homes, taverns and sports stadiums.

Americans and millions of others around the world still watch the Super Bowl in anticipation of seeing that year's big Budweiser and Bud Light commercials. And each time they see one, they probably say to themselves, "Anheuser-Busch, St. Louis, Missouri."

BY EVAN S. BENN

The sprawling, red-brick campus of the Anheuser-Busch InBev brewery sits at Broadway and Pestalozzi Street just south of downtown St. Louis.

Here's a look at some of A-B's most memorable ad campaigns over the years:

Spuds MacKenzie (1987): This lovable bull terrier with a brown patch of fur around its left eye was the embodiment of a "party animal" in its time as Bud Light's mascot. Spuds, who was actually a female named Honey Tree Evil Eye, donned sunglasses, fraternity T-shirts and leather jackets as part of A-B's print and television spots.

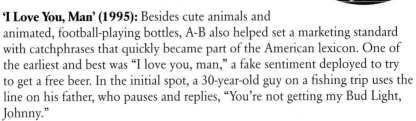

Bud Bowl (1989): An animated feature that aired during halftime at the Super Bowl, the Bud Bowl pitted a team of Budweiser bottles against a lineup of Bud Light bottles in a mock game of football. No matter what brand "lost," A-B had a winning tradition for the Bud Bowl's eight-year run.

'I Love You, Man' (1995): Besides cute animals and animated, football-playing bottles, A-B also helped set a marketing standard with catchphrases that quickly became part of the American lexicon. One of the earliest and best was "I love you, man," a fake sentiment deployed to try to get a free beer. In the initial spot, a 30-year-old guy on a fishing trip uses the line on his father, who pauses and replies, "You're not getting my Bud Light, Johnny."

Bud-Weis-Er Frogs (1995): The "talking" bullfrogs that croaked "Bud" …
"Weis" … "Er" became an instant hit after their Super Bowl debut. Consumers
loved the ads, which racked up a number of industry awards. But some parents
groups complained that the frogs were aimed at marketing beer to kids, a
similar criticism that came up during the Spuds MacKenzie era.

BY EVAN S. BENN

Visitors are greeted by the classic A-B logo before touring Anheuser-Busch InBev in St. Louis.

'Whassup?' (1999): One of the Internet's first viral-video obsessions, the "Whassup?" commercials were widely quoted, imitated and parodied for years to come. The comical catchphrase was credited with helping Budweiser experience an uptick in sales for the first time in almost two decades.

Real Men of Genius (2000): "Here's to you," the ads began, then went on to mock-extol the virtues of dubious achievements. Odes to Mr. Beach Metal Detector Guy, Mr. Boneless Buffalo Wing Inventor and Mr. In the Car Nose Picker were among the more than 160 spots that aired on radio and TV, accompanied by background vocals from former Survivor front man David Bickler.

'Dude' (2007): The brewery's biggest hit ad in more than five years featured beer-drinking dudes responding to various situations with different inflections of one simple word: Dude. The popular TV spot also was an Internet sensation, attracting more than 15 million views.

Here We Go (2010): Responding to slumping sales, A-B moved away from its "drinkability" campaign with Bud Light when it unveiled "Here We Go" as the brand's tagline in 2010. The line was intended to convey Bud Light as a catalyst for good times.

All beers, regardless of style, fall in one of two categories: lagers and ales. Lagers (including pilsners and Oktoberfests) are produced with bottom-fermenting yeasts brewed at a lower temperature than ales (including pale ales and stouts), which are created with top-fermenting yeasts at warmer temperatures.

BEER SLOGAN QUIZ

Match these timeless slogans with the beers they advertised:

1. **Hooray beer!**

2. **It works every time.**

3. **The Champagne of beers.**

4. **It's what your right arm is for.**

5. **Probably the best beer in the world.**

6. **The beer that made Milwaukee famous.**

Quiz answers

1. Red Stripe   2. Colt 45   3. Miller High Life   4. John Courage Beer   5. Carlsberg   6. Schlitz

BY EVAN S. BENN

GENTLE GIANTS

Hitches of towering Clydesdale horses are one of the longest-running and most iconic symbols of Anheuser-Busch in St. Louis.

Two stables here – on the brewery campus and at Grant's Farm, about 10 miles southwest of A-B – house a few dozen of the more than 200 Budweiser Clydesdales that are spread throughout the country and travel to parades, sporting events and celebrations.

Here are some quick facts about the "gentle giants":

• Budweiser Clydesdales typically weigh about 2,000 pounds, stand 6 feet at their shoulders, are bay in color and have white-stocking feet.

• Clydesdales can eat up to 60 pounds of hay and drink 30 gallons of water a day.

• Clydesdale horseshoes are 20 inches long and weigh 5 pounds each.

• Their handcrafted, brass-and-leather harnesses and custom-fitted collars weigh about 130 pounds.

• The brewery's first Clydesdales, a six-horse hitch, were a gift presented in 1933 to August A. Busch Sr. from his sons August A. Busch Jr. and Adolphus Busch III to commemorate the repeal of Prohibition.

• A Dalmatian has been the Clydesdales' symbol since 1950. One now rides behind every hitch in the famous red, white and gold beer wagons, next to the driver.

More information: anheuser-busch.com/historyClydesdales.html, grantsfarm.com

RECYCLABLE ART

Anheuser-Busch InBev, the Boston Beer Co. and other breweries have used the work of Fenton, Mo., artist Michael Halbert on their beer labels. He created artwork that appears on the label of Michelob Ginger Wheat, which was released for the first time in 2010.

Fenton, Mo., artist Michael Halbert knows that some of his best work winds up in people's recycling bins.

Halbert has made a career out of illustrating beer labels. His work currently appears on beers and packaging from brewers such as Anheuser-Busch InBev, MillerCoors and Samuel Adams, so there's a good chance that if you'd had a bottle of beer or bought a six-pack in recent years, you've owned a piece of Halbert's art.

"A couple of times at bars, I would go up to people who were drinking a particular bottle and say, 'Hey, I made that illustration,'" says Halbert. "I don't do that anymore."

Halbert specializes in scratchboard – a technique in which the artist etches black-and-white images into a clay board, giving an old-time, engraved-wood appearance. Breweries' design firms hire him to draw wheat strands or hop vines or malted grains for labels, packaging and advertisements.

BY EVAN S. BENN

Several beers from Anheuser-Busch's Michelob Brewing Co. contain Halbert's label art, including one of its recent seasonal beers, Michelob Ginger Wheat. Halbert created the knuckle of ginger in the label's foreground and the wheat in its background.

"The goal is to develop a label and packaging with an appealing look that clearly communicates the beer's attributes," says Nate Scudieri, a Michelob brand manager. "Beer enthusiasts want to know a lot about the beers they enjoy, which is why we put details about the beer's style and ingredients on the actual label."

Beer labels have a "huge effect" on consumers because they influence purchasing decisions from store shelves to bar menus, Washington University marketing professor Joseph Goodman says.

"At a grocery store, we look to labels for information about what's in the product; but at a bar, a beer label doubles as an advertisement, which makes it incredibly important," Goodman says. "We're more likely to buy what other people are buying, so if you see someone else drinking a certain beer, that's going to influence you."

Even breweries without the marketing budgets of A-B InBev and MillerCoors recognize the importance of having labels that stand out.

"Beer labels … help attract people for the initial purpose, and if the nectar is good, they'll come back for more," says Chris Lennert, vice president of Left Hand Brewing Co. His Colorado craft brewery rolled out all new labels for its beers in 2010.

Halbert didn't become an artist to help create beer labels. In fact, when he started back in the late 1970s, he wanted nothing to do with beer.

"My wife was very religious and did not drink, so by extension, neither did I," Halbert explains. "The company I was working for at the time did a lot of ad work for Anheuser-Busch, but I told my boss I didn't want to work on that account."

Halbert eventually split with his wife and started taking on work from beer companies. Since then, he's sold thousands of the scratchboard illustrations that he creates in a cramped studio off his bedroom. Besides the work he's done for beer companies, Halbert's art has appeared on book covers, wine labels and airline television commercials.

Not bad for a college dropout from Potosi, Mo., who worked on the assembly line at the old Chrysler plant in Fenton while building his art portfolio.

| CHAPTER 3 | # SCHLAFLY BEER |

NEW KIDS ON THE BLOCK

The year was 1991. The Soviet Union collapsed. Ah-nold said "I'll be back" in "Terminator 2: Judgment Day." Nirvana set the decade's rock tone with its smash-hit grunge album "Nevermind," and boy band New Kids on the Block topped Forbes' list of highest-paid entertainers.

St. Louis had its own new kid on the block that year. For the first time in more than half a century, a new production brewery opened in the city. The Schlafly Tap Room at 2100 Locust Street, toward the western edge of downtown, became an instant hit from its first night, Dec. 26, 1991. St. Louis Brewery co-founders Tom Schlafly and Dan Kopman poured their Schlafly Pale Ale that night, which remains the brewery's flagship beer.

People thought the lawyer (Schlafly) and the brewer (Kopman) with a fondness for British ales were crazy for trying to sell their beer in the shadow of "the brewery." A-B at that time had a 44 percent market share of all U.S. beer sales and an even greater slice of the St. Louis pie. But finding demand has never seemed to be a problem – keeping up with it was the issue.

Sales of Schlafly beer grew by double digits every year after the Tap Room opened. To keep the beer flowing, the brewery outsourced production to Minnesota, where Schlafly's bottled beers were contract-brewed starting in 1996. That all changed when the company opened its Schlafly Bottleworks in Maplewood in 2003 (on the 70th anniversary of the repeal of Prohibition).

Every 12-ounce bottle of Schlafly beer and most kegs are brewed and filled at Bottleworks, which oversees more than 20 styles of beer every year. On a busy day, Bottleworks' 25 production workers will fill about 2,000 cases and 300 kegs. St. Louis Brewery's annual output has more than doubled since Bottleworks opened, from just under 15,000 barrels in 2004 to about 35,000 barrels in 2010. (Worth noting: A-B InBev's St. Louis brewery is capable of cranking out 35,000 barrels in a day.)

St. Louis Brewery co-founder Dan Kopman, seated at left, samples beer with employees at his Schlafly Bottleworks brewpub in Maplewood in 2008. The facility has undergone recent expansions to keep up with demand for its many styles of Schlafly beer.

A recent $3 million Bottleworks expansion has pushed St. Louis Brewery's annual capacity to 45,000 barrels. The original Schlafly brewhouse at the Tap Room is still going strong, producing a few dozen types of beer each year for the brewpub and distribution that include Belgian-style ales, an oak-aged barleywine, a bourbon-barrel-aged imperial stout, special-release beers in 750-ml bottles, cask-conditioned ales and wild-yeast beers that will age for years in wood barrels in the Tap Room's underbelly.

Besides being a workhorse of a brewery, Bottleworks boasts an organic garden, plays host to a year-round farmers market and – like the Tap Room – serves up some of the area's most respectable pub fare along with live music many nights. The food menus reflect the different vibes of the two brewpubs. The Tap Room offers British-style comfort staples like exemplary fish 'n' fries and steaming bowls of curry mussels, while Bottleworks veers toward suburban-hippie chic with its vegetarian black-bean burger and baked bread made with spent brewing grain.

Schlafly Tap Room chief brewer Stephen Hale oversees the St. Louis Brewery's barrel-aging program. Here, he stands on barrels that previously held Jim Beam whiskey but now are filled with Schlafly Reserve Imperial Stout, letting the beer soak up subtle flavors of bourbon and oak.

To celebrate the 30,000th barrel of Schlafly beer brewed in 2009, St. Louis Brewery co-founder Dan Kopman taps a special keg while his business partner Tom Schlafly, right, and longtime Schlafly Tap Room bartender Kevin Nash look on.

Much has changed in the 20 years since Tom Schlafly and Dan Kopman took the bold step of opening a brewery on the King of Beer's home turf. Schlafly says people told him he was out of his mind for doing such a thing – even he likened the move to starting a new religion in Mecca. Now that his beer is sold in more than a half-dozen states (and available at Busch Stadium – no small feat), it's hard to question Schlafly's success. The brewery he and Kopman started in 1991 paved the way for St. Louis' beer resurgence and set the standard by which other craft breweries here are measured.

(Another change since 1991: beer prices. That's why beer drinkers in the know flock to the Schlafly Tap Room on the day after Christmas. Every Dec. 26, the brewery throws itself a birthday party with all beer prices rolled back to what they were in 1991 – about $3 a pint.)

One thing that hasn't changed is the misconception that Schlafly and other craft brewers are waging a David-vs.-Goliath battle against the Big Breweries like A-B and MillerCoors. That story line heated up again after InBev's 2008 takeover of A-B. Almost overnight, the makers of Schlafly beer had the new title of St. Louis' largest locally owned brewery.

But the biblical anecdote doesn't tell the whole story, as Schlafly Bottleworks head brewer James "Otto" Ottolini explained:

"The David/Goliath reference has been used so many times to compare Schlafly to A-B. David slew Goliath. We have no plans or intentions to slay A-B. If we use the David and Goliath story at all, it would be using the example of how David played on his own terms and pressed forward when it seemed pointless. The point I am making is that we want to sell great craft beer. That can and will happen in a market where A-B InBev rules the roost. It doesn't inherently make us enemies. I have a lot of respect for how they do things as well as for the beers they make."

Tom Schlafly also notes that respect and appreciation between his brewery and A-B outweigh any actual competition.

"In one sense, there's competition," Schlafly told the Post-Dispatch. "But not really. That's like saying my softball team is competition for the Cardinals. We've benefited from being near them because they've made a great name for brewing in St. Louis."

HOW MUCH BEER IS IN A BARREL?

Barrels are units of measurement that breweries use to keep track of how much beer they make and sell. A barrel consists of 31 gallons of beer. That's enough beer to fill about 330 12-ounce bottles (about 14 cases) or to pour about 200 20-ounce drafts. Most metal beer kegs that you may have seen behind bars or at college frat parties are called "full kegs" or "half barrels" and contain 15.5 gallons of beer. Schlafly brewed about 35,000 barrels in 2010. That's 1,085,000 gallons, or about 11,550,000 12-ounce bottles.

WHAT IS CASK-CONDITIONED BEER?

Sometimes called cask ales or cask-conditioned beers, these are unpasteurized brews left to age or "condition" in vessels called casks. The beer develops natural carbonation in the cask and is poured without added carbon dioxide pressure, as typical kegged beers are. Cask ale should be served at cellar temperature, about 54 degrees, which is several notches warmer than the frosty draft beers many of us are used to. This allows the beer's nuances to come alive, releasing more fragrant hop aromas and fuller flavors.

Some of the better beer bars around town will host occasional cask nights (download the P-D's free Hip Hops beer app at stltoday.com/beerapp to keep up on the latest St. Louis beer news and events), and the Schlafly Tap Room always has two cask-conditioned beers flowing. For a neat experiment, ask for a pint of Dry-Hopped APA from the regular draft system and one from the cask. Prepare for your mind to be blown when you see how different cask ale can be.

STEPHEN HALE AND JAMES "OTTO" OTTOLINI, SCHLAFLY HEAD BREWERS

Before he became a professional brewer, Stephen Hale spent time as a chimney sweep, a sea-urchin diver, a classical-studies major and a Latin teacher. James "Otto" Ottolini was an electrician's apprentice in high school who went on to earn a degree in French and, more recently, an MBA from Washington University's Olin Business School. Together, the men oversee St. Louis Brewery's brewing operations, Stephen at the Schlafly Tap Room downtown and Otto at Schlafly Bottleworks in Maplewood.

Stephen Hale

Stephen is a native of Maine who has been brewing Schlafly beer almost nonstop since the earliest days of St. Louis Brewery. Besides his on-the-job training, Stephen has honed his craft at the Siebel Institute of Technology, a world-renowned beer school. And he credits much of his knowledge and skill to fellow pro brewers and homebrewers alike. You can spot Stephen at the Tap Room and around town in his signature Utilikilt – a modern workman's take on the Scottish style.

James "Otto" Ottolini

The equally affable Otto, a lifelong St. Louisan, also landed at the Schlafly Tap Room soon after it opened, first getting hired on the restaurant side. A homebrewer with an interest in food, Otto uses both a baker's precision and a chef's improvisational touch in his approach to beer. He soon found a home on the brewing side of St. Louis Brewery, going on to become head of brewery operations and No. 1 brewer at Schlafly Bottleworks.

PRESENT

Ryan Northcut installs beer tap handles at the International Tap House in Chesterfield.

BY EVAN S. BENN

CHAPTER 4

NOT SO MICRO

THE RISE OF CRAFT BEER

Every craft beer drinker remembers their gateway beer. That's the one that led to an "Aha!" moment, causing the person to pursue microbrews and abandon flavorless macro lagers. Pioneers of the American craft-beer revolution converted legions of new fans in the 1980s and '90s with brews like **Samuel Adams Boston Lager, Sierra Nevada Pale Ale** and **Widmer Bros. Hefeweizen,** all of which remain top sellers in the craft segment. The beer landscape began a glacial shift as homebrewers opened their own microbreweries and more people clamored to seek out their beers. The boom of new, small, regional breweries – as opposed to the long-standing, massive-scale, international behemoths like A-B, Miller and Coors – caused the rise of the term "craft brewery" to describe independent beermakers that didn't rely on adjunct ingredients like corn and rice to lighten their beers' flavor or appearance.

Craft breweries and brewpubs have seen unprecedented growth in recent years, with more than 1,700 operating in this country at the start of 2011. St. Louis has certainly contributed to the trend. The number of breweries and brewpubs within a two-hour drive of downtown is approaching 20 – more than the area has seen since before Prohibition. Most of those have come online in the past 10 years.

After St. Louis Brewery formed in 1991, the next big splash in the local craft-beer production market came from O'Fallon Brewery. Husband-and-wife owners Tony and Fran Caradonna opened their brewhouse in 2000 in an industrial area about 35 miles northwest of downtown St. Louis. O'Fallon built its business on its flagship **Gold,** a golden ale with a similar appearance and alcohol content as Budweiser, but has gained fans through its more unusual beers like **Smoked Porter** and **Cocoa Cream Stout. O'Fallon Wheach,** a wheat beer with peach flavor that comes out every spring, has become synonymous with warm weather in St. Louis.

BY EVAN S. BENN

O'Fallon Brewery brewmaster Brian Owens uses a paddle to stir barley and hot water in a mash tun. The resulting liquid is known as wort, which will be fermented into beer.

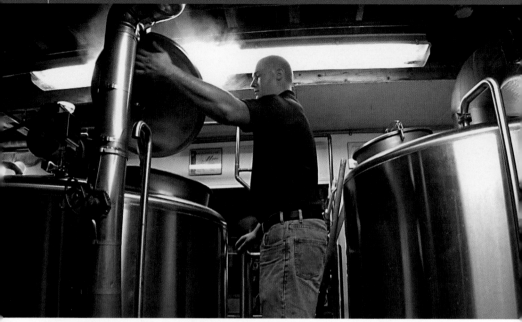

Brewer Marc Gottfried works on a batch of Honey Wheat beer at Morgan Street Brewery & Restaurant on Laclede's Landing downtown in 2009, right around the time that craft beer really began its boom in St. Louis.

Success of St. Louis' two main craft breweries helped bolster other brewpubs throughout the area. Morgan Street Brewery & Restaurant on Laclede's Landing specializes in traditional lagers, including an award-winning **Golden Pilsner** that is now distributed to other local bars and restaurants. Square One Brewery & Distillery uses ingredients like maple syrup, sour cherries and agave nectar to add a unique dimension to the beers it serves at its Lafayette Square brewpub. Trailhead Brewing Co. matches classic styles like stout, brown ale and amber ale to its family-oriented food menu in historic St. Charles. Buffalo Brewing Co., located in Midtown Alley near St. Louis University's campus, serves up an impressive array of house-brewed beers to go with its bison-heavy menu.

Despite the surging popularity of craft-made brews, those products account for less than 5 percent of all beer consumed in the United States. Will craft beer ever turn the tide and replace light lagers as the fizzy beverage of choice for U.S. adults? Brewers sure hope so, but until that happens, they say they will continue to put out boundary-pushing beers that are big on flavor.

BY EVAN S. BENN

"Beer is a multibillion-dollar industry," says Phil Wymore, who moved to St. Louis from Chicago in 2010 to start Perennial Artisan Ales with his wife and father-in-law. "Craft brewers don't expect to take that entire pie. We're just hoping to get a slice of it by making the best beer we can."

WHAT IS CRAFT BEER?

The Boulder, Colo., based Brewers Association defines craft breweries as small, independent and traditional companies that produce fewer than 6 million barrels of beer a year. The term "microbrewery" now refers to small operations that brew fewer than 15,000 barrels of beer a year. Want to go even smaller? "Nanobrewery," used to describe extremely limited-production craft brewhouses, seems to fit somewhere between homebrewing and microbrewery.

THE THREE-TIER SYSTEM

After Prohibition, lawmakers enacted a "three-tier system" for the distribution of alcoholic beverages in the United States. Although exact laws vary from state to state, Missouri follows the basic three-tier system that includes producers, wholesale distributors and retailers. The producers (breweries) can only sell their beer to wholesalers, which in turn sell the beer to retailers (restaurants, bars & liquor stores), which can then sell it to consumers. Some critics complain that the system has allowed big breweries to unfairly dominate distribution channels and therefore monopolize shelf space and tap handles on the retail level. A 2009 documentary, "Beer Wars," examines the three-tier system in detail, including how it affects craft breweries like Delaware's Dogfish Head and California's Stone.

IB-Who? IBUs, or International Bittering Units, is a scale that measures the bitterness of a beer based on its hop additions. The higher the IBU, the more bitter or hoppy the beer.

CRAFT BEER, DEFINED

The Brewers Association, a Colorado-based advocacy group, defines craft breweries as "small, independent and traditional." Here are the group's criteria:

Small • A craft brewery's annual production is 6 million barrels of beer or fewer.

Independent • Less than 25 percent of a craft brewery is owned or controlled by an alcohol beverage industry member who is not a craft brewer.

Traditional • Craft breweries must produce an all-malt flagship or have at least 50 percent of their volume in either all-malt beers or in beers that use adjuncts to enhance rather than lighten flavor.

CRAFT BREWERIES' FLAGSHIP BREWS

Here are four of the beers that helped establish St. Louis' craft-beer resurgence:

Schlafly Pale Ale • British hops and a London ale yeast create a copper-color brew with both a mild hop spiciness and a bready malt sweetness. At 4.1 percent alcohol by volume and a bold yet smooth flavor, Schlafly Pale Ale is truly a "gateway" beer that can turn people on to the complexities of craft brew.

Morgan Street Golden Pilsner • Morgan Street brewmaster Marc Gottfried's recipe for this Bohemian-style pilsner has won awards at major national brewing competitions. That should come as no surprise to anyone who's tried it – Golden Pilsner is clean, medium-bodied and leaves a gentle hop bite on the palate. Ask St. Louis brewers their favorite locally made beer, and odds are good that they will cite Golden Pilsner.

BY EVAN S. BENN

O'Fallon Gold • This appropriately named golden ale is brewed with two varieties of hops and three kinds of malted barley, then filtered for a clean hue and crisp, refreshing flavor. Gold was O'Fallon's first beer and remains a top seller, even though the brewery has expanded its portfolio to include an India pale ale and chocolate, peach and pumpkin beers.

Trailhead Red Amber Ale • Original Trailhead brewmaster John Witte drew up the recipe for this brew based on an American craft-beer classic: Sierra Nevada Pale Ale. Piney and citrusy hops from the U.S. Northwest provide the backbone for Trailhead Red's heady aroma and full flavor.

Jeff Britton from Wentzville, Mo., the president of the Garage Brewers Society, sports a hops tattoo while loading hops into what he calls a "hop infuser" during the St. Louis Brewers Heritage Festival in Forest Park.

BY EVAN S. BENN

HOMEBREWING IN ST. LOUIS

St. Louis' proud brewing tradition naturally extends to a talented community of homebrewers. Thousands of men and women here with an affinity for beer and a knack for the science behind it spend their nights and weekends perfecting an India pale ale recipe or sourcing orange peels for their next witbier. Several clubs and supply stores in the area (see links at end) ensure that these enthusiasts can share their knowledge with each other and keep up with the best equipment.

Here is a look into the home-brewing prowess of a few St. Louisans:

Don Loeffler started making beer for economic reasons, but his homebrewing hobby soon turned into a matter of taste.

"I thought, 'I like beer. If I brew my own, I can make it for three bucks a six-pack,'" he said. "But once you brew your own and compare it to the quality of stuff you find in the supermarket, everything else tastes like watered-down Kool-Aid."

Loeffler and his fiancée, Laurie Jacobson, joined the ranks of St. Louis-area homebrewers in 2009. He's retired with a background in marketing and engineering; she's an accomplished home cook who likes to tinker in the kitchen. They were looking for something they could enjoy together.

The wet bar in the basement of their Chesterfield, Mo., home doubles as a bottling line.

"Our very first batch was a nut brown ale, and everyone raved about it – neighbors, friends, our kids," Loeffler said. "We just got hooked. We found this really neat community here of folks who brew their own beer, and we haven't looked back."

St. Louis homebrewers are among the most active and organized in the country, with at least four clubs whose members meet regularly to critique each others' creations and to offer help and equipment to novices.

"It's a real friendly atmosphere here," said Dan Stauder, a past president of St. Louis Brews, one of the larger clubs. "Our more experienced brewers are always willing to help out the newer brewers, show them different ways to set up their brewing systems."

The systems run the gamut from fairly simple kits available online for less than $30 – Loeffler and Jacobson boil some ingredients in a soup pot on their stove, siphon it into bottles and let the natural sugars and yeast do their magic – to complex setups that require elaborate equipment, precise science and all-grain ingredients.

"One guy I work with is trying to create an 80-gallon boil pot," Stauder said. "With homebrewing, it's sort of like the sky's the limit in terms of what you want to do."

Stauder started brewing in college and now serves as a professional homebrew judge. He said his club's membership had more than doubled in recent years. St. Louis Brews has 140 participants, most of whom meet once a month at the Missouri Beverage Co. Members range from 21 to 93 years old.

"It's not just about the beer and the alcohol," Stauder said. "A lot of us love the technical process behind it. We've got mechanics and machinists who like to build stuff; biologists who like to play with temperatures and chemistry; and we've got schoolteachers, police officers, doctors and lawyers. It's one of those things that offers something for everybody."

Several St. Louis home-brewers have gone on to create beer professionally for the area's craft brewers, Anheuser-Busch or breweries in other states.

One who bridges the gap between amateur and professional is Jim Yeager, a homebrewer who moved to St. Charles County about four years ago after a stint in France. He tried making his own wine but found himself growing restless during the months-long fermentation. When he learned that beer takes only two or three weeks from start to finish, "it didn't take long for brewing to become the main focus," he said.

Bob Yeager, left, and his brother Jim taste beer samples at a monthly meeting of the Garage Brewers Society homebrew club at O'Fallon Brewery in O'Fallon, Mo.

Yeager started attending meetings of St. Louis Brews and another big club, Garage Brewers Society, which meets monthly at the O'Fallon Brewery. One of the recipes he crafted – a hoppy, crisp amber ale – impressed O'Fallon brewmaster Brian Owens enough that they collaborated to create a beer for the Pro-Am competition at the 2009 Great American Beer Festival in Denver.

Yeager took a day off from his job as a client finance manager at IBM to help O'Fallon's brewers make the beer, which they called **Alright Already Amber** and put on tap at a few places around town, including the International Tap House in Chesterfield. Yeager didn't expect it to win any national awards.

"By this point, I had brewed one of my beers on a commercial system, had sold it locally and received a ton of compliments on it, so I was already thrilled," he said.

But at the beer festival, Yeager's thrill grew when judges awarded Alright Already Amber a silver medal – second place out of 72 entries.

"It didn't really compute," he said of the moment the award was announced. "My wife was shaking me, saying, 'That's you! That's you!' And then they put it up on the screen for everyone to see. At that point, I was pretty sure I wasn't dreaming."

Maybe one day, Loeffler and Jacobson will create their own recipes and enter their brews in competitions. But for now, they're content with experimenting in small batches, sharing tips and trading equipment with other homebrewers, and enjoying their homemade beer.

They've made nine batches since they started – about 540 bottles – and they're not likely to go to a grocery store for a beer run anytime soon.

"You could go buy a six-pack for $8, but I don't see the point," Loeffler said. "Quite honestly, I like mine better."

WANT TO BREW?

The St. Louis area is home to several homebrewing clubs that welcome new members. Here are four to check out:

St. Louis Brews • stlbrews.org

Garage Brewers Society • garagebrewers.com

East Side Brewers • eastsidebrewers.org

Master Brewers Association of the Americas • mbaastl.com

HOMEBREW SUPPLY SHOPS

St. Louis Wine and Beermaking, 231 Lamp & Lantern Village, Chesterfield. wineandbeermaking.com

Worm's Way Garden and Homebrew, 1225 North Warson Road, St. Louis. wormsway.com/Missouri.aspx

Dave's Homebrewing Supplies, 122 East Main Street, Belleville. Ill. daveshomebrewgourmet.com

CHAPTER 5 | WINE COUNTRY

NOT IN THE MOOD FOR WINE? NO PROBLEM

On a brisk afternoon in Ste. Genevieve, Mo., Tony Saballa, the winemaker and brewmaster at Charleville Vineyard Winery & Microbrewery, helped a local hog farmer hitch a wagon of spent brewing grains onto the farmer's truck.

"He feeds it to his pigs after we use it in the brewing process," Saballa said. "It leaves here like that" – mushy brown stuff – "and comes back as bacon."

That's the kind of keep-it-local philosophy that has guided Saballa and Charleville's owners since they added a brewhouse to their winery in late 2004. Charleville's lineup of beers is bottled and labeled one at a time, by hand, and is available in grocery stores, beer shops and restaurants from St. Louis to Cape Girardeau, Mo.

Right • The great arbor of the Jean Baptiste Valle House contains the original grapevines planted by the family of the last French commandant in Ste. Genevieve, Mo. The vines were planted more than 200 years ago.

BY EVAN S. BENN

The entrance to Charleville Vineyard Winery and Microbrewery in Ste. Genevieve.

"We have capacity to make 1,500 barrels," said Saballa, who brewed about a third of that in 2009. "But it's not like a do-or-die thing to get there. We take it one day at a time."

In 2011, Weingarten Vineyard is opening a 20,000-square-foot facility at 12323 State Road 32 in Ste. Genevieve, with several beers made on-site.

Saballa oversees Charleville's labor of beer love with assistant brewers Dave "Panda" Scarmana and Tait Russell, who is the son of Charleville's owners, Jack and Joal Russell. They've come up with a variety of interesting yet easy-to-drink beers, including the red-hued, slightly sweet **Tornado Alley Amber Ale** and a floral, hop-forward American IPA called **Hoptimistic.**

Just up the wine trail from Charleville, another Missouri winery has gotten into the beer act. Crown Valley Brewing and Distilling Co. produces a rotating selection of about 10 beers for sale around the state and at its on-site taproom and beer garden.

BY EVAN S. BENN

Crown Valley's brewmaster, Carl Wiersma, learned beer in Wisconsin before joining Anheuser-Busch as a brewhouse manager and sensory director in charge of training professional beer tasters. Since Wiersma helped Crown launch its beer program, the brewery has released classic lagers and both American and Belgian-style ales. A Crown favorite around St. Louis is **Plowboy Porter,** a smooth and creamy dark brew with chocolate notes from its roasted malts.

Crown and Charleville's brews have become such a hit that people are traveling to wine country for beer. Crown now offers a Pub Club, giving members first dibs on things like seasonal releases and tickets to an annual brewmaster's dinner.

The bar inside Crown Valley Brewing and Distilling Co. in Ste. Genevieve.

Visitors to Charleville Winery and Microbrewery do their tasting in a rustic setting.

By Evan S. Benn

Overlooking Charleville's 14-acre vineyard with a silky, nitrogen-carbonated Oatmeal Stout in hand, Saballa said he never forgets how fortunate he is to have the freedom to make beer and wine in such a beautiful setting. He's the type of brewer who still cares enough about his product to cringe when he reads a negative review on a site like Beer Advocate.

"Some people see the words 'Winery and Microbrewery' on our labels and say, 'I wish the wine guys would stick to wine,'" said Saballa, who started as a homebrewer in California and perfected the craft at Chicago's world-renowned Siebel Institute. "It's frustrating because this is who I am. It's what I love to do."

The rolling hills of Crown Valley Winery at sunrise.

BY EVAN S. BENN

For more information:

charlevillevineyard.com

crownvalleybrewery.com

HAVE A BEER

Here are a few favorites from Charleville and Crown's lineups:

Crown Plowboy Porter • Roasted malts give off aromas of cocoa powder and caramel, which lead to similar flavors of coffee and chocolate. Pleasantly zippy carbonation keeps this dark beer from being too heavy.

Crown Horseshoe Pale Ale • An American-style pale ale, Horseshoe is neither overwhelming nor wimpy – an excellent gateway to the world of craft beer. Brewed with American Cascade hops, the beer emits bright citrus aromas and flavors.

BY EVAN S. BENN

Charleville Half-Wit Wheat • The best of Belgium and American wheat beers combine in this tasty hybrid brewed with wheat, ground coriander and oranges. Half-Wit is endlessly refreshing on a hot day.

Charleville Box of Chocolate • This winter-seasonal release is a rich brew with loads of chocolate flavors. A hint of banana esters from Belgian yeast provide a flavor of chocolate-covered bananas.

CHAPTER 6 | # LOVE FOR LOCAL

BREWERS SHARE THEIR ENTHUSIASM

Brewers are invariably enthusiastic about what they do, and it shows. These tireless men and women wake up before dawn, don rubber boots and spend the bulk of their days doing janitorial work: sanitizing equipment, hosing down the brewhouse, cleaning out kegs and fermentation tanks.

But they wouldn't trade the life for anything; in fact, many professional St. Louis brewers had previous careers, as veterinarians, architects, winemakers, pizza cooks, Latin teachers, engineers and more, before turning to brewing full-time.

Grrrrowler:
Not every local brewery puts its beers in bottles or cans, but most will sell you a growler to take home. What's a growler, you ask? It's a half-gallon glass container that keeps draft beer fresh for a few days. And it'll make you the hit of a party if you show up with a few in hand.

And besides loving what they do, brewers have a profound respect for their craft, and for others who practice it. It's not uncommon in St. Louis for the same brewer to work shifts in three different breweries. It's also not uncommon for a brewer to call upon a competitor for a spare bag of malt or help scoring some extra hops. The camaraderie they share doesn't end at the day-to-day tasks – it extends to the finished product.

We asked several St. Louis brewers about local beers that they love or that have inspired them. Here's what they had to say.

JOSH WILSON, FERGUSON BREWING CO.

My biggest influence probably would have to be **Square One's Imperial Pilsner.** It was my first real brew that I got to help with before I became a brewer. (Square One brewmaster) John Witte let me tag along for that batch and, in a way, became my mentor when it came to brewing. It was a pretty cool experience going up to Square One after the beer was ready and having all my friends up there with me to try it.

(Another) has to be **Schlafly Pale Ale.** It was the first craft beer I ever tried. I'm pretty sure that I wasn't even old enough to be drinking yet, but someone let me try it, and I remember it being the exact opposite of what I thought beer was supposed to taste like and thinking it was the most bitter thing ever. Now I have to look back and laugh at my ignorance and be thankful that there are so many good beers out there to try.

JOHN WITTE, SQUARE ONE BREWERY & DISTILLERY

In about a six-month period from 1987-88, when I was just getting into beer and before I started homebrewing, I had three beers that really changed my perspective: **Coors Winterfest, Anheuser-Busch Märzen** and **Samuel Adams Boston Lager.** It was sort of this incremental process of discovering what beer could be. I remember having that Märzen at a place in Ballwin, Mo., and it was phenomenal.

John Witte

I have a lot of respect for Marc Gottfried's **Morgan Street Golden Pilsner.** That beer has won several awards recently, including a gold medal at the World Beer Cup. That is impressive, having your Bohemian-style pilsner go up against pilsners that are actually from Bohemia – and winning.

EVAN HIATT, SIX ROW BREWING CO.

(When) I was living in Cape Girardeau, **Charleville** was one of the few readily available local craft brews, one of which was their **Hoptimistic IPA** – nicely balanced with great hop character and body. Definitely one of the first beers to open my eyes to identifying and using American hop varieties.

TONY SABALLA, CHARLEVILLE VINEYARD & MICROBREWERY

I'm a big fan of what now may be coined as the classics or standards, so I always look to **Morgan Street Brewery** for a rock-solid **Golden Pilsner.** This brewery, in my opinion, is often overlooked and offers down-to-earth beers for both the beer novice and beer lover.

MARC GOTTFRIED, MORGAN STREET BREWERY & RESTAURANT

I'm a huge fan of **O'Fallon Wheach.** I am not usually a fruit-beer fan, but that stuff is the ultimate in the summertime.

Marc Gottfried

BRIAN OWENS, O'FALLON BREWERY

I enjoy a good Bohemian pilsner, and one of the first and best versions of the style that I had was **Morgan Street's Golden Pilsner.** It is a medium-bodied pils with nice malt complexity balanced with a spicy hop finish. With all of the choices of beers to drink these days, Marc Gottfried's Pilsner is one I always fall back on because it is such a quaffable sessioner and one I remember trying when I was really starting to discover craft beer years ago.

Brian Owens

STU BURKEMPER, O'FALLON BREWERY

Mine is, honest to God, **O'Fallon Gold.** First craft beer I ever had and first time I had ever heard of O'Fallon Brewery.

JAMES OTTOLINI, ST. LOUIS BREWERY (SCHLAFLY BOTTLEWORKS)

Dave Johnson's **Rye IPA** at **Buffalo Brewing Co.** is awesome. Dave is the James Brown of the St. Louis brewing community. He is everywhere. Chances are good in St. Louis that if you drink a great beer, Dave had a hand in making it.

Brian Owens does a great job at O'Fallon. I love **O'Fallon Pumpkin Ale.** We have our own version, but they make a great pumpkin beer.

Marc Gottfried is a child prodigy of brewing. While most kids were practicing Big Wheel stunts, or trying to figure out how to get their hands on a fake ID, Marc was concerned with brewing science. **Morgan Street's Golden Pilsner** rocks.

James Ottolini

BY EVAN S. BENN

Florian Kuplent translated into English means "excellent beer." I can't wait for his creative expressions at **Urban Chestnut** to find their way to my imbibing apparatus.

DAVE JOHNSON, BUFFALO BREWING CO., HIGHLANDS BREWING CO.

Back in the early '80s, **Michelob Dark** was basically my gateway beer. If a bar had it on tap, that was what I was drinking. It is, or is similar to, **AmberBock.** I don't know if they just changed the name, but I had a lot of it.

STEPHEN HALE, ST. LOUIS BREWERY (SCHLAFLY TAP ROOM)

Inspiration has come from many brewers and breweries around the world, but also from a very local source: **homebrewers.** There are many excellent craft brewers among us in St. Louis, and we're all further enriched by the dedication of so many talented homebrewers in our broader beer community.

As a former quasi-regular member of the **St. Louis Brews** and getting to know many of the brewers involved with the **Garage Brewers Society** and the **East Side Brewers,** and having started my brewing career more than one-and-a-half score years ago, I owe much to the world of homebrewing. Changes have been abundant in this world: availability of ingredients and advances in equipment are obvious, but information exchanges in this modern world have accelerated the pace at which one can advance as a homebrewer. In short, the homebrewing community is one of the most inspirational sources for new beer styles.

FLORIAN KUPLENT, URBAN CHESTNUT BREWING CO.

One of my local favorites is the **O'Fallon Smoked Porter.** I love smoked beers, and I think that this is a very nice example of the style.

Florian Kuplent

EVAN'S PICK 7

St. Louis Beers That Should Be in Your Fridge or Cellar

Key
D = Drink now
C = Cellar
D/C = Drink now or cellar

CHARLEVILLE BOX OF CHOCOLATE (D/C)

Recently rebranded (its old name, Double Chocolate Belgian Quad, was a mouthful), this high-alcohol (10.5 percent ABV) dessert sipper from Charleville Vineyard Winery & Microbrewery in Ste. Genevieve, Mo., is a luscious display of rich milk chocolate. I swear it tastes like chocolate-covered bananas. This bottle's a good candidate for the cellar if you can find any, or be ready to try it fresh upon its release around Valentine's Day.

MICHELOB PORTER (D)

St. Louis' most consistent year-round porter in a bottle, Michelob Porter is better than most people probably give it credit for. With soft flavors of coffee, chocolate and caramel from roasted malts, which become more pronounced as the beer warms up, this is a good way to convert people who have convinced themselves they don't like "dark" beers.

O'FALLON GOLD (D)

This lightly hopped, clear golden ale has been O'Fallon Brewery's flagship product since it launched in 2000. It's smooth, refreshing and not at all heavy or overpowering. Gold is an ideal session beer that is a mainstay of fridges throughout St. Louis and beyond.

O'FALLON SMOKE (D/C)

One of the best-kept local beer secrets is O'Fallon Smoke, a world-class smoked porter made in our backyard. Judges deemed it perfect enough to be a gold-medal winner at the 2004 Great American Beer Festival. And I humbly agree. It's smoky like a campfire but approachable enough to drink year-round.

SCHLAFLY DRY-HOPPED APA (D)

This hoppy dream was the first St. Louis craft beer I fell in love with. Three varieties of U.S. hops go into this American pale ale, which may very well be my desert-island beer among this list. Thank goodness for the folks at Schlafly who put a Brewed On date on every bottle – as with all hoppy beers, this one is best fresh, so check that date before you buy.

SCHLAFLY PUMPKIN ALE (D/C)

It's been well documented that I prefer O'Fallon's fall-release pumpkin beer by a hair over Schlafly's. That said: Schlafly Pumpkin Ale earns a spot on this list because, with a higher alcohol content (8 percent) than O'Fallon's, it's a better candidate for cellaring. And if you buy, say, a six-pack this year, and you stash away a few bottles, then you do the same thing next year and the year after that, you'll be able to have a pretty cool three-year vertical tasting party. This beer's flavors develop, change, mellow and enhance over time. Experiment by tasting multiple vintages. Have fun.

SCHLAFLY RESERVE IMPERIAL STOUT (C)

The last time I tasted side-by-side samples of several vintages of this superb brew (circa summer 2010), the 2007 version stood out for its exemplary flavors of vanilla and cola. But what's brilliant about this bourbon-barrel-aged beer is how well it ripens in a cool, dark place. Maybe next time I try it, the 2007 vintage will be past its prime but the 2010 version will be bursting with chocolate and bourbon goodness. Either way, this is a bottle worth picking up every year.

| CHAPTER 7 | # THROW A PARTY |

GOOD BEER AND GREAT TIMES

When Tom Schlafly and Dan Kopman started the St. Louis Brewery – maker of Schlafly beer – in 1991, their mission was simple: Make good beer and throw really good parties.

More than two decades later, the beer's still flowing, and the party hasn't stopped. The brewery's two locations – the Tap Room downtown and Bottleworks in Maplewood – play host each year to more than a dozen festivals, parties and other excuses to drink beer, eat food and listen to live music.

Some of the events are eclectic (Scottish poet Robert Burns' birthday is memorialized every January with a reading by Tom Schlafly and heaping plates of haggis), while others are epic (autumn's Hop in the City and spring's Stout & Oyster Festival are not to be missed). But they all combine good beer and great times, which is to say the brewery continues to succeed on its original mission.

Shane Hale plates up his competition pork steaks for the Brew and Q World Pork Steak Championship sponsored by Schlafly.

But Schlafly isn't the only beer-slinger in town who knows a thing or two about throwing raucous parties.

Urban Chestnut Brewing Co. celebrates hops from the world's largest hop-growing region – Hallertau, Germany – at HopfenFest in spring at its midtown location. The Stable, Amalgamated Brewing Co.'s Benton Park brewpub, gets into the Halloween spirit each October with its Monsters of Beer event, bringing in kegs of high-alcohol craft brews from around the country.

BY EVAN S. BENN

Tim Young, of O'Fallon, Mo., and Carol Lagana of Pevely dance at the St. Louis International Beer Festival, held at the World's Fair Pavilion in Forest Park.

Glassware:

Beer served in almost any vessel – from a red Solo cup to a Riedel wine glass – is a pleasurable experience. But no matter what you drink out of (my preference is a thin-lipped tulip glass or a laser-etched globe glass from New Belgium Brewing Co.), make sure it's clean. And whatever you do, please don't freeze it before using.

St. Louis also is home to no fewer than three big annual beer festivals, each of which gives beer enthusiasts and newcomers alike the chance to sniff, sip and savor to their heart's content. Don't want to drive? Don't worry – each event provides discounted or free tickets for designated drivers, so you can bring someone to make sure you get home safe.

In addition to the big festivals, St. Louis Craft Beer Week plays an integral role in the local beer community, organizing tastings, TweetUps, beer dinners and more. The events are spread throughout the city and county (as well as the East Side), giving everyone a chance to take part in the best our local breweries, restaurants and beer bars have to offer. To keep up with the latest: stlbeerweek.com.

Workers prepare the arched entranceway to the St. Louis Brewers Heritage Festival in Forest Park. The yearly summer event brings together local breweries to pour their best beers for thousands of thirsty festival-goers.

ST. LOUIS BREWERS HERITAGE FESTIVAL

Matt Cartier of Augusta, Mo., sips a beer at the St. Louis Brewers Heritage Festival.

As the name suggests, this festival, usually held in June at Forest Park's central fields, celebrates the area's brewing history and the camaraderie of its current lot of brewers. Festival-goers can sample beers from just about every brewery in town, from Anheuser-Busch to the little guys, as well as from the region's premier homebrewers. What's especially cool: The commercial brewers pick one style of beer and each brew their own versions of it, so drinkers can taste how different brewing systems and ingredients can alter the profile of the same type of beer.

More info • stlbrewfest.com.

BY EVAN S. BENN

ST. LOUIS MICROFEST

From left, Marla Warren of St. Charles, Theresa Hlavinka of Clayton and Collen Villagomez of St. Louis share a laugh over beers at St. Louis Microfest, an annual craft-beer festival in Forest Park.

Also at Forest Park, this springtime fest features hundreds of beers from craft producers, both domestic and international. Microfest's lineup also includes brewer demonstrations and talks from chefs about how to pair beer and food. Live music from local acts and food from area restaurants make Microfest a premier kickoff to summer.

More info • stlmicrofest.org.

ST. LOUIS CENTENNIAL BEER FESTIVAL

Started by a few friends as a way to fill a slow weekend before the Super Bowl, January's Centennial Beer Festival has grown into a yearly tradition for many in St. Louis. Held at the Moulin event space under Vin de Set restaurant, this fest includes multiple beer-tasting sessions as well as an exclusive brewmaster's dinner that is a sellout every year.

More info • centennialbeerfestival.com.

BEER FESTIVALS 101

Tiffany Tillotson of Jonesburg and Micah Irish of Wentzville sample brews at the St. Louis Brewers Heritage Festival.

The people-watching at beer festivals never ceases to entertain: college bros double-fisting cigars and beers; dads pushing baby strollers with a milk bottle in one cup holder, a beer glass in the other; newbies asking for "something Corona-y," eliciting laughter from a beer geek with a necklace made of hard pretzels.

Clearly, some people have more beer-fest experience than others. It's understandable that the situation can be intimidating. There are hundreds of beers from dozens of breweries near and far. So how do you know where to start: Ale or lager? Dark or light? Familiar favorite or first-time taste?

Here are some pointers.

BY EVAN S. BENN

FIRST FLIGHT, LOW AND LIGHT

Nothing will overwhelm your taste buds and ruin your ability to taste — and think — clearly like starting with a hugely hopped and high-alcohol India pale ale. Just like at a wine tasting, it's best to begin by sampling lighter-bodied and lower-alcohol choices. It helps to have at least a basic knowledge of beer styles, so you'll know to go for things like pilsners, brown ales and wheat beers before IPAs, stouts and double bocks.

Serving temp: Forget what you've heard about beers needing to be frosty-cold. Beer served at too-cold temperatures lose all the aroma and flavor nuances that make drinking it so enjoyable. Most beers hit their sweet spot around 45-55 degrees. Don't be afraid to let your beer warm for a few minutes out of the fridge!

SNIFF, SIP, SAVOR, REPEAT

Once you've got a few ounces of liquid in your glass, evaluate the brew the way beer judges (and writers) do: Look at it, smell it, sip it. Does the beer look cloudy or clear? Is it golden or black or something in between? Does the carbonation produce a foamy head or leave a thin lacing at the top?

Steve Franz of St. Charles waits for a pour of Anheuser-Busch InBev's Landshark Lager at the 2009 Beer & Brats Festival at West Port Plaza.

BY EVAN S. BENN

Erin Allan of Manchester tries to balance beer at St. Louis Strassenfest at Chesterfield's Central Park in 2009.

Next, give the beer a swirl and put your nose close to it. Beers give off a range of aromas, from fresh-cut grass to molasses. What do you smell?

Now the fun part: drinking. Swish the beer in your mouth so it hits all of your taste-bud sensors. Can you taste bitterness (from hops) and sweetness (from malts)? Are they balanced, or does one overwhelm the other?

SPIT BUCKETS ARE YOUR FRIEND

You would be surprised how quickly the alcohol in 2-ounce samples can catch up to you. You'd also be surprised at how many beers you thought would be great but end up being disappointing.

Don't be ashamed to use the spit buckets stationed near every table. If you feel like one sip is enough but still have more in your glass, dump the rest into the bucket and move on.

BY EVAN S. BENN

On a similar note, use the water pitchers at the tables to give your glass a rinse between beers; it'll help ensure that you get the aromas and flavors the brewers intended.

HYDRATE

I don't want to sound like your mother here, but daytime, outdoor drinking is a recipe for dehydration if you're not careful. Plus, water helps keep your palate fresh. Check to see if you can bring your own water bottle into the event. Otherwise, pony up a few bucks for water at the concession stand.

DRINK OUTSIDE THE BOX

Before you fall into your comfort zone of drinking beers you know and love, do yourself a favor and try some that are new to you.

As much as I want to race right over to the Schlafly, O'Fallon and New Belgium tables, those are beers I can reach for any time. Instead, I first try beers from brewers that don't distribute in Missouri or from local brewpubs with new batches to sample.

Cyndee Strickland of St. Charles hoists a brew at the Beer & Brats Festival at West Port Plaza.

CHAPTER 8 | # BEER IS FOOD

RESTAURANTS FOCUS ON FOOD

One sign of St. Louis' growing appetite for craft-made beer is that chefs and restaurant owners are getting into the mix in a major way. Beer dinners, where restaurants collaborate with breweries to pair food with different beer styles, have become regular fixtures at many eateries around town, from humble taverns to upscale bistros. The quality and length of beer lists at restaurants is continuing to improve as chefs realize that beer can complement and elevate their food in a way that's every bit as good – if not better – than wine. Even grocery stores have caught on to the craft-beer wave, stocking bigger and better selections than ever before. This marriage of beer and food is encouraging people to experiment with more than the plain-old lager and pizza (although those two *do* go very well together). In this chapter we'll highlight how beer is finding an expanded role in restaurants, grocery stores and home kitchens.

CRAFTING A RESTAURANT BEER LIST

Until recently, this was a common scene at many St. Louis restaurants: I'd thumb through a multipage wine list – from $30 California whites to $500 Tuscan reds – searching in vain for beer.

I'd know I was in trouble when a look of surprise, then confusion, came over a server's face before he scurried off to the bar to inquire about beer. He'd return with disheartening but predictable news: The options were mostly limited to a few domestic light lagers.

For a long time, beer has taken a back seat to wine at restaurants. But that's changing, thanks to a growing appreciation from chefs and diners of how well beer can pair with food. In the past few years, the St. Louis area has seen the birth of several restaurants that take beer seriously: Brasserie by Niche, Bridge, the Good Pie, Pi and Peel, to name a few.

Here are some of the elements I look for in a restaurant's beer offerings. I hope owners take heed and make some room on their menus for quality beer – I think they can find space on the page with the super Tuscans.

Steamed clams go great with Morgan Street Steam beer.

SELECTION

"The key to a successful beer list is having a well-rounded selection that matches nicely with your food," says Coby Arzola of Pi Pizzeria. "For us, that means a mix of wheat beers, hoppier beers and some German-style lagers."

Arzola oversaw an expansion of Pi's beer program in 2010 that increased the tap handles at its Delmar Loop location to 20 from 12. Also in the works are plans to offer beer dinners, cask nights and flight specials.

Coby Arzola

"The whole beer-and-food movement is really heading in the right direction," Arzola says. "People who enjoy good food tend to have good taste in beer, too, so we want to give them lots of choices."

SEASONALITY

Brasserie in the Central West End shows its beer-first mentality on the food menu: Six seasonally changing draft beers are printed on the front; you have to flip it over to find the wine.

"A beer list should rotate with the seasons, just like food," says STL Hops blogger Mike Sweeney, who worked as a consultant in helping Brasserie sculpt its beer offerings.

In the warmer months, Brasserie swaps out the malty, burnt-sugary **St. Bernardus Prior 8** dubbel – a perfect match for winter stews and root vegetables – for the lighter, crisper **St. Bernardus Witbier.** The keg space that **Schlafly Winter ESB** occupied in the winter typically contains the St. Louis Brewery's **Helles-Style Summer Lager** by June.

SUPERMARKETS AND RETAIL SHOPS WITH BIG BEER SELECTIONS

The Schnucks supermarket in Des Peres has one of the best beer selections of any grocery store in the area, with many of its 315 brands of beer kept in a 38-degree walk-in cooler near the cheese and wine department.

Not too long ago, the options in most supermarket beer aisles were limited to products from the big breweries. If you were lucky, maybe you'd find some **Sierra Nevada** or **Samuel Adams** offerings tucked away on a shelf corner.

But as demand for craft beer continues to grow, grocery stores are upping their game so customers don't have to make an extra trip to a specialty shop for great beer.

"Grocery stores always adjust to what the consumer wants, whether it's beer or cheese or deli meats," says Brian Dix, who oversees the beer division of local distributor Major Brands. "The consumer has found a taste for craft beer, so that's been gaining more shelf space."

Besides the added convenience of being able to do your beer shopping and food shopping in the same place, grocery stores also tend to have longer hours of operation and more locations (although selection varies from store to store) than beer-and-liquor shops.

The Schnucks Des Peres store that opened in 2009 on Manchester Road stocks about 315 beers. Most of them are stored in a walk-in cooler in the middle of the store that's kept "at a balmy 38 degrees," jokes department manager Matt Wider, a 36-year Schnucks veteran.

"Customers like to experiment with different beer styles and flavors to match food combinations, so people have been asking for all kinds of varieties," Wider says, adding that **Schlafly, New Belgium, Bell's** and **O'Fallon** beers are among the store's best-selling craft brews. "We've really been trying to pick up the rare stuff from breweries that may only send 30 or 50 cases to the entire state."

The Brentwood Whole Foods is sort of like my secret beer stash because it often carries special releases that may have already sold out or aren't available at other places around town, including **Founders KBS, The Fish Guy's Wild Ass Amber Ale** and **Charleville's St. Dorian Abbey Rye.**

Runner-up honors go to Dierbergs at Telegraph Plaza in Oakville, Trader Joe's at Brentwood Promenade and Shop 'n Save in O'Fallon, Mo.

That Dierbergs location is a standout among the chain's St. Louis stores in terms of beer selection, stocking a good supply of domestic and export craft brands.

And TJ's, while it doesn't refrigerate its beers, offers can't-beat values on popular craft suds as well as on its own private-label brews. You have to experiment for yourself to see which of the latter suit your palate; I don't care for **Frugal Joe's Ordinary Beer,** but I think the **Mission St. Brown Ale** (brewed by Firestone Walker) and the winter-release **Trader Joe's Vintage Ale** (brewed by Unibroue) are full-flavored winners.

Or, if you're feeling adventurous, grab a "Mystery Six-Pack," a brown-bagged sixer with beers that the store's employees have selected for you. It's a great way to uncover some gems that you might not have otherwise picked up.

The O'Fallon Shop 'n Save at 1421 Mexico Loop Road East is one of the grocery chain's newest and biggest stores, many of which offer a good range of beers at very competitive prices.

STYLE

In many ways, offering a smart mix of beer styles is more important than having a huge selection. For Brasserie, Sweeney focused on French and Belgian styles like biere de garde **(Castelain Blond, Jolly Pumpkin Oro De Calabaza)** and saison **(Boulevard Tank 7)** to pair with French and Belgian food.

"Those are just fantastic, all-purpose beers that have spicy components and enough effervescence to lift away fattiness from duck, pork, chicken, anything," he says.

SUGGESTIONS

I give bonus points to any restaurant that suggests beer pairings next to its menu items. It helps people who might be apprehensive about trying a new beer the same way they might be with a wine made from a grape that's difficult to pronounce.

Did you know?
Cenosillicaphobia is the fear of an empty glass.

For that reason, it's perfectly acceptable for a restaurant to keep a few staple beers that are fallbacks for customers. That's why, on Brasserie's bottled beer list, a $3 **Budweiser** is listed along with a $14 **New Belgium Le Fleur Misseur** (22 ounces). At Pi, they take a different approach to customer satisfaction.

"People come in and ask, 'Where's the **Bud Light**?'" Arzola says. "It's our job to say, 'Well, we don't have that, but here's a taste of **Schlafly Kolsch** or **New Belgium Blue Paddle Pilsner.** Try it; you might like it.'"

PLACES TO GO

A selection of (non-brewpub) St. Louis-area restaurants with impressive beer lists:

BIGELO'S BISTRO
140 North Main Street, Edwardsville, Ill.

BLUEBERRY HILL
6504 Delmar Boulevard

BRIDGE
1004 Locust Street

CICERO'S
6691 Delmar Boulevard

DRESSEL'S
419 North Euclid Avenue

BY EVAN S. BENN

ECLIPSE
6177 Delmar Boulevard

FARMHAUS
3257 Ivanhoe Avenue

THE GOOD PIE
3137 Olive Street

IRON BARLEY
5510 Virginia Avenue

MILAGRO MODERN MEXICAN
20 Allen Avenue, Webster Groves

PEEL
921 South Arbor Vitae, Edwardsville, Ill.

PI
6144 Delmar Boulevard; multiple locations

HOME COOKING WITH BEER

Cooking with beer – as an ingredient, not just a treat for the cook – is one of the best ways to spotlight the beverage's versatility and draw out its elemental flavors.

It's a pity, then, that so many mainstream cookbooks and recipes rarely get more specific than suggesting using "beer," which is about as helpful as calling for a cup of vegetables or a tablespoon of dairy.

Different styles can impart varying qualities to your dish, so it's important to find recipes that specify particular beer types or to experiment until you discover what beer works best.

I once tried using a hoppy India pale ale in the braising liquid for beef brisket. The long cooking time concentrated the hop bitterness into a harsh, astringent-tasting flavor that did the meat no favors.

Instead, I've found that malt-forward lagers like **Samuel Adams Boston Lager, Shmaltz Coney Island Lager** and **Yuengling Lager** (Yuengling's not available in Missouri or Illinois) are excellent choices. They lend a caramelized sweetness and roasted nuttiness that play off the salt and richness of the meat.

For a twist, I made the brisket recipe with **Schlafly Pumpkin Ale.** Its spicy cinnamon and clove elements mellowed during the long braise, giving the meat and sauce a deep flavor that ground spices alone might not have achieved.

Despite my failed IPA brisket experiment, hoppy beers do have a place in the kitchen. A recipe for roasted-garlic IPA mashed potatoes is one that has serious crossover appeal from beer fans to foodies.

Sean Paxton, who created the dish for his site, homebrewchef.com, says almost any IPA will do, but he goes so far as to recommend ones brewed with Summit or Columbus hops, which have an earthiness (some describe Summit hops as "oniony") that complements the roasted garlic.

The beer – only a few tablespoons – is added at the end of the cooking process, to layer in some extra flavor. This allows the pungent hops to shine without having to worry about them turning acrid like in the brisket incident.

Also, because you'll have the better part of a bottle to finish, choose a beer that you enjoy drinking. **Avery DuganA,** a double IPA made with Columbus hops, is a good choice; local favorite **O'Fallon 5-Day IPA** contains Summit hops and works in this dish.

Few beer-and-food marriages are more harmonious than mussels steamed in white ale or witbier, a style that is traditionally brewed with coriander and orange peel. Instead of the (equally delicious) buttery lemon broth that results from using dry white wine, using white ale creates a heady bouquet of spice and citrus.

Mussels have a quick cooking time, which means whatever beer you choose will retain many of its original flavors. **Hoegaarden Original, Ommegang Witte** and **New Belgium Mothership Wit** all serve double duty in this dish — you can cook with them and pair them with the final product.

For a variation on the coriander-and-orange flavors of witbiers, a friend grabs a growler of **Square One Brewery's Spicy Blonde** whenever he's about to steam mussels. The Belgian-style ale is spiced with ginger and lemongrass, giving the dish a Southeast Asian flavor.

Dessert courses also provide opportunities to incorporate beer. At a Hip Hops beer-and-cupcakes pairing event, baker Melissa Manaois whipped up a frosting using **Founders Breakfast Stout** to top chocolate chip mocha cupcakes.

I used a bottle of **Left Hand Fade to Black Vol. 2** — a smoked Baltic porter — and chocolate coffee "bark" from St. Louis chocolatier Kakao to make a batch of ice cream. Fade to Black's smoky elements were well-hidden, letting the beer's dark-chocolate and black-coffee flavors mingle with the decadent, vanilla-spiked cream.

Just about any stout or porter would work in that ice cream or in Manaois' frosting, but look for ones with especially pronounced coffee and chocolate: **Southern Tier Mokah, Schlafly Coffee Stout, Lagunitas Cappuccino Stout.**

CHAPTER 9 | # SENSATIONAL SUDS

A GUIDE TO ST. LOUIS' BREWPUBS

For some places, the intersection of food and beer is a natural fit. Brewpubs make both under the same roof, meaning you'd be hard pressed to find fresher suds to go with a plate of food anywhere else.

More than a dozen brewpubs – places that brew and sell their own beer and serve a full menu of food or light snacks – operate within a 30-minute drive of downtown St. Louis.

Skinny Minnie: Most 12-ounce American pale ales and lagers contain fewer calories than an equal-size serving of 2-percent milk or orange juice.

The granddaddy of the bunch is the St. Louis Brewery's Schlafly Tap Room, a downtown fixture since 1991 that continues to brew some of the city's most innovative and flavorful beers. (Cask-conditioned Schlafly American Pale Ale is a perfect match for the city's best plate of fish-n-chips.)

Sensational suds also are available beyond the city's limits. From Ferguson to Kirkwood to St. Charles, craft beer is flowing like never before. Here's a guide to what's out there:

BY EVAN S. BENN

Customers partake in the "10 flight draft beer sampler" at the Highlands Brewing Co. in Kirkwood, Mo.

BY EVAN S. BENN

AMALGAMATED BREWING CO.: THE STABLE

1821 Cherokee Street, Benton Park • thestablestl.com • 314-771-8500

The vibe • A converted Lemp Brewery horsey home, the cavernous Stable can get boisterous when filled with patrons who come for events such as weekly Beer Bingo and occasional cask-beer nights. Most seats in the house are within view of the brew kettles and stills used to make the Stable's Amalgamated beers and distilled spirits.

What to drink • German-style lagers **Zoigl** and **Helles** are standouts thanks to Amalgamated brewer Augie Altenbaumer.

What to eat • Pizzas with any toppings you want and meaty burger-grinders rarely disappoint. Feeling adventurous? Try the "Plate of Food": chef's choice, $9, no refunds.

The Stable in Benton Park gets its name from its former life as a stable for Lemp Brewery's horses.

By Evan S. Benn

Assistant brewer Ashleigh Arnold works in the brewing room, with an open view of the Stable's bar.

BUFFALO BREWING CO.

3100 Olive Street, midtown • buffalobrewingstl.com • 314-534-2337

The vibe • Nestled in the same complex as Pappy's Smokehouse, Buffalo attracts students from nearby St. Louis University and craft-beer fans, who come for the respectable burgers and Dave Johnson's superfresh brews.

What to drink • Rye IPA, an India pale ale brewed with a healthy amount of rye grain, is a favorite whenever it's on tap.

What to eat • Lean buffalo meat is the name of the game here. Go for a buffalo burger or the beef-and-bison meatloaf.

Server Mandy Dabbs, center, checks on a table of customers at Buffalo Brewing Co., a brewpub in St. Louis' Midtown Alley.

BY EVAN S. BENN

FERGUSON BREWING CO.

418 South Florissant Road, Ferguson • fergusonbrewing.com • 314-521-2220

The vibe • North St. Louis County residents and beer lovers from across the region have flocked to Ferguson's only brewpub since owner Joe Lonero opened it in April 2010. He changed the name from Hill Brewing Co., but the food, dozen or so homemade brews and happy-hour specials remain the same.

What to drink • Brewed with real nuts, **Pecan Brown Ale** has a delicately nutty flavor that complements the brewpub's smoked foods.

What to eat • Long-cooked items including smoked chicken wings and Cajun-style jambalaya are menu highlights.

Ferguson Brewing Co. in downtown Ferguson features great beers, a beer-mug-shaped bike rack and a fake rooftop palm tree.

BY EVAN S. BENN

A bartender pours a fresh pint of beer for a customer at Ferguson Brewing Co., which also offers to-go growlers, kegs and an array of smoked-meat dishes.

Inside the Ferguson Brewing Co.

By Evan S. Benn

HIGHLANDS BREWING CO.

105 East Jefferson Avenue, Kirkwood • highlandsbrewing.com • 314-966-2739

The vibe • Located in the heart of downtown Kirkwood, Highlands is a destination for live music and karaoke, as well as for its sizable pub-food menu (including one for the kids) and approachable beer styles.

What to drink • Blackberry Wheat, Highlands' best-selling beer, has a discernible blackberry flavor and refreshing wheat zip, and it's about to be distributed for the first time to other bars and restaurants around town.

What to eat • You'll want that beer to cool off your palate after a buffalo chicken wrap or chipotle barbecue pork flatbread pizza.

Growlers line the bar at Highlands Brewing Co. in Kirkwood.

BY EVAN S. BENN

Lead singer Frankie Muriel of band Dr. Zhivegas rocks out during a performance at Highlands.

Kate Bacon pulls a draft beer for a customer among Highlands Brewing Co.'s 10 housemade beers. The brewpub's Blackberry Wheat is its best seller.

BY EVAN S. BENN

MORGAN STREET BREWERY & RESTAURANT

721 North Second Street, Laclede's Landing • morganstreetbrewery.com • 314-231-9970

The vibe • A little college sports bar-y with plenty of banquet space for private parties, Morgan Street is the place to go on the Landing for craft suds.

What to drink • Brewmaster Marc Gottfried's award-winning **Golden Pilsner** has won the hearts of beer judges, fellow brewers and droves of beer drinkers.

What to eat • For a lunch bite on the Landing, portobello salad with goat-cheese croutons is a sure bet.

Morgan Street Brewery on Laclede's Landing downtown has begun to distribute kegs of its flagship Golden Pilsner to bars and restaurants throughout St. Louis.

By Evan S. Benn

BY EVAN S. BENN

Morgan Street brewmaster Marc Gottfried (shown on previous page in a 1999 photo and here in 2009) checks on a batch of his Honey Wheat beer at the Laclede's Landing brewpub.

ST. LOUIS BREWERY: SCHLAFLY BOTTLEWORKS

7260 Southwest Avenue, Maplewood • schlafly.com/breweries • 314-241-2337

The vibe • Clean and tidy (it has to be – it's where the brewery produces its bottled Schlafly beers), Bottleworks also has an organic, laid-back feel thanks to performances by bluegrass groups and the farmers market it hosts weekly during the growing season and monthly through winter.

What to drink • Your favorite Schlafly beer. Whatever it is – **Pale Ale, Hefeweizen, Oatmeal Stout, Pilsner** or various seasonal selections – odds are it's on tap and ultrafresh.

What to eat • Quite possibly the best black-bean burger in town is served here, topped with smoked Gouda cheese and a spicy sriracha aioli.

With more than 10 beers on tap at any time, it's hard not to find something tasty to pair with food at Schlafly Bottleworks in Maplewood.

BY EVAN S. BENN

James "Otto" Ottolini watches as a new fermenting tank is lowered into Schlafly Bottleworks, where he serves as head of brewing operations.

St. Louis Brewery added four 200-barrel fermenting tanks to its Schlafly Bottleworks facility in 2010 to keep up with demand, increasing its capacity by 13,000 barrels of beer a year.

By Evan S. Benn

ST. LOUIS BREWERY: SCHLAFLY TAP ROOM

**2100 Locust Street, downtown • schlafly.com/breweries
• 314-241-2337**

The vibe • A St. Louis institution for 20 years, the Tap Room, with its wooden floors and tables and the aromas of a place where beer is made and consumed, is home to several legendary things: Schlafly beer (obviously), addictive Sticky Toffee Pudding and an unbeatable plate of fish-n-chips.

What to drink • Cask-conditioned beer. Options usually are a hopped-up **Schlafly APA** (American pale ale) or whatever else the brewers are playing with that particular week.

What to eat • A recent menu update added some satisfying items like a lamb burger, gravy- and cheese-curd-smothered poutine, and heaping bowls of mussels. But don't try to lure us away from the fish-n-chips: beer-battered and fried cod, salty French fries and tangy tartar sauce.

The Schlafly Cod & Cask Festival is one of the brewpub's most popular annual parties. Here, Schlafly Tap Room's Matt Mulholland prepares a 45-pound piece of cod in 2006. It made the record books as the largest plate of fish and chips in Missouri history.

"Mad scientist" Schlafly Tap Room brewer Brennan Greene experiments by pouring a fresh Schlafly beer over ice cream for a unique float.

BY EVAN S. BENN

Brewer Brennan Greene checks the inside of an oak barrel formerly used for aging bourbon before filling it with Schlafly Imperial Stout in the cellar at the Tap Room on Locust in St. Louis. Greene and chief brewer Stephen F. Hale, left, will fill 32 of the bourbon barrels with the stout beer, then let them sit for anywhere from two weeks to two months to absorb flavor.

SIX ROW BREWING CO.

3690 Forest Park Avenue, midtown • sixrowbrewco.com • 314-531-5600

The vibe • Friendly, attentive bartenders, a low-key atmosphere and high-quality beers have helped Six Row build a solid reputation.

What to drink • Want something that's punch-you-in-the-face hoppy? Try brewmaster Evan Hiatt's **Double IPA.** Feeling more like something sessionable for a night out with friends? Go with **Whale,** Six Row's light but flavorful wheat-pale ale hybrid.

What to eat • We're not saying it would pass muster at the Carnegie Deli, but the piled-high pastrami sandwich on Six Row's expanded food menu hits the spot.

A sampler flight like the one seen here is one of the best ways to experience the beers offered at Six Row Brewing Co.

Thanks to its clean, friendly atmosphere
and quality beers, Six Row Brewing Co. has
quickly become a favorite in Midtown Alley.
A full food menu supplements multiple beer
taps, as well as select wines and spirits.

By Evan S. Benn

SQUARE ONE BREWERY & DISTILLERY

1727 Park Avenue, Lafayette Square • squareonebrewery.com • 314-231-2537

The vibe • The front bar area takes center stage for socializing and drinking brewmaster John Witte's creations, while tables in the dining room and outdoor patio fill up with couples and families looking for a meal.

What to drink • Witte frequently changes the dozen or so styles he brews for Square One, so it's hard to know what will be on the draft list from week to week. **Park Avenue Pale Ale** is an excellent introduction to the world of craft beer; in the summer, **Agave Wheat** is a thirst-quenching favorite.

What to eat • Flank-steak nachos with grilled corn salsa is perfect sharing food. For bigger appetites, most entree options come with suggested beer pairings.

Jessica Jaeger of Richmond Heights enjoys a laugh and a beer at the bar of Square One Brewery & Distillery in Lafayette Square.

BY EVAN S. BENN

Square One's patio is a cozy spot nestled off Park Avenue in Lafayette Square.

Bartenders fill drinks at Square One Brewery & Distillery, seen here from a window to the brewpub's outdoor patio.

By Evan S. Benn

TRAILHEAD BREWING CO.

921 South Riverside Drive, St. Charles • trailheadbrewing.com • 636-946-2739

The vibe • Trailhead is a perfect place to stop for a bite and a pint after an afternoon strolling on St. Charles' historic Main Street. Catch the best deals during weekday happy hour from 4 to 7 p.m.

What to drink • Trust your brewer. Go with the seasonal Brewer's Selection. From the year-round lineup, **Trailhead Red Amber Ale** will please fans of Sierra Nevada Pale Ale.

What to eat • Open-face prime rib sandwich with melted cheese on an onion roll.

Jennifer Muckerman of Trailhead Brewing Co. empties grain from a mash tun in this 2010 photo.

BY EVAN S. BENN

Jennifer Muckerman checks on a batch of beer at Trailhead Brewing Co. in St. Charles.

URBAN CHESTNUT BREWING CO.

3229 Washington Boulevard, midtown • urbanchestnut.com • 314-222-0143

The vibe • Urban Chestnut is a brewery first and foremost, but co-founders Florian Kuplent and David Wolfe are showcasing Kuplent's creations in a relaxed bar area and outdoor beer garden with some snacks. The tasting room is open 11 a.m.-midnight from Tuesday-Saturday.

What to drink • Half Crown is Urban Chestnut's idea of a "session IPA," meaning it has the dry-hopped aroma and flavor of an American India pale ale but with a restrained alcohol content. About a half-dozen other beer styles join it on tap.

In their words • "Florian and I hope to contribute to the already-vibrant local craft beer culture. It is a great time for beer in St. Louis." – Wolfe

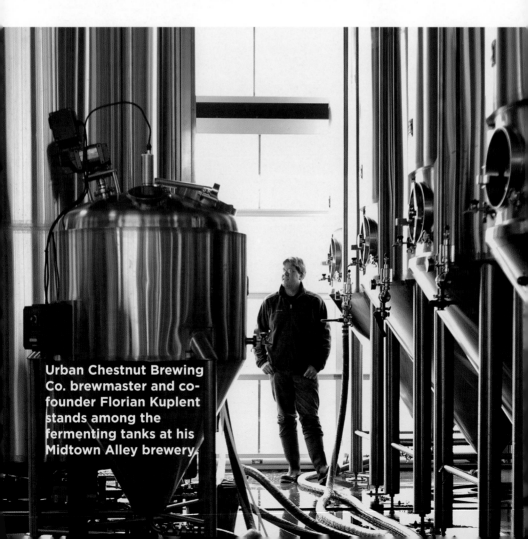

Urban Chestnut Brewing Co. brewmaster and co-founder Florian Kuplent stands among the fermenting tanks at his Midtown Alley brewery.

David Wolfe, the
co-founder of Urban
Chestnut Brewing Co.

By Evan S. Benn

Florian Kuplent inspects equipment at Urban Chestnut Brewing Co., which he co-founded in 2011 with David Wolfe.

BY EVAN S. BENN

PERENNIAL ARTISAN ALES

8125 Michigan Avenue, South Carondelet • perennialbeer.com

What's on tap • Brewmaster and owner Phil Wymore is planning to keep a dry-hopped, **Belgian-style pale ale** and a **saison** available year-round. He also wants to put a different beer style on tap every month at his tasting room. Pie lovers, get ready: The first one he's considering is a **strawberry-rhubarb witbier.**

In their words • "We want to be a part of this craft brewing revolution that can make St. Louis a prominent beer destination like Seattle, Portland, Denver (and) San Diego." – Wymore

Perennial Artisan Ales founder and brewmaster Phil Wymore stands in front of his new brewery on Michigan Avenue in St. Louis' South Carondelet neighborhood.

THE CIVIL LIFE BREWING CO.

3714 Holt Avenue, Tower Grove South • thecivillifebrewingcompany.com

What's on tap • Brewmaster Dylan Mosley, who has been working on the brewery's concept with Civil Life founder Jake Hafner for several years, says the first few beers they'll produce for distribution and their tasting room are an **American brown ale,** a **rye American pale ale** and a **British-style special bitter.**

In their words • "Our tasting room is inspired by the parts of my life that have been spent working in or drinking in bars from St. Louis to New York to Belgium, England, Germany, Czech Republic, Poland and all those places in between. But most importantly, it will be uniquely ours and uniquely American." – Hafner

The Civil Life Brewing Co. owner Jake Hafner, shown here and at right, helped transform a former newspaper-distribution warehouse in St. Louis' Tower Grove South neighborhood into a brewery.

FUTURE

CHAPTER 10 · PAGE 136

MORE ON THE WAY

New breweries are popping up all over town.

The beer tanks in the basement production area of Six Row Brewing Co. in St. Louis.

CHAPTER 11 · PAGE 142

WHAT'S NEXT

Let's look into our crystal ball and predict what's coming in the world of craft beer.

APPENDIX · PAGE 152

RESOURCES

Brewery contact and tour info, a style glossary and reference materials to aid your quest for beer knowledge.

CHAPTER 10 # MORE ON THE WAY

A BREWING REVOLUTION CONTINUES

St. Louis is awash in new breweries, with several opening in the past two years and more expected to open by the end of 2011.

And they're not being run by sharks simply looking to cash in on craft beer's surging popularity. The owners and brewmasters of these small operations are passionate about their craft, which they've worked years to hone.

Florian Kuplent and David Wolfe opened **Urban Chestnut Brewing Co.** in the city's Midtown Alley in early 2011. Kuplent, a German-born master brewer, and Wolfe, a marketing expert, worked for years at Anheuser-Busch before deciding to go out on their own. The tasting room adjacent to their brewery was an immediate hit, thanks in large part to Kuplent's beers, which run the gamut from old-world, traditional lagers to boundary-pushing ales.

Florian Kuplent

David Wolfe

As Kuplent and Wolfe readied to open their doors, a flurry of other new-brewery announcements made St. Louis beer drinkers salivate in anticipation.

Phil Wymore, who grew up in Missouri and majored in anthropology at Mizzou, learned about brewing in Chicago, where he attended the Siebel Institute, a prestigious beer school. From there, he brewed professionally at Goose Island and Half Acre Beer Co., finding a knack for Belgian-style and barrel-aged beers. He moved to St. Louis in 2010 to start **Perennial Artisan Ales,** which he is opening with his wife and father-in-law in a former Coca-Cola syrup plant in the South Carondelet neighborhood.

Phil Wymore

"We view St. Louis as one of the best markets to start a brewery due to the explosion of craft beer culture in the city – in the form of breweries, beer bars, festivals, etc.," says Wymore, who hopes to focus some of Perennial's production on sour beers, a category that's gaining favor among craft-beer drinkers.

"We'll experiment with adding sour and funky notes to different styles of beers and play around with various sugar sources to feed the yeasts — especially seasonal fruits."

Jake Hafner, a culinary school graduate who ran one of St. Louis' most popular wine bars for eight years, spent a good part of 2009 canvassing Europe's pub culture. When he returned to St. Louis, Hafner knew he wanted to open a brewery and tasting room that celebrated good beer and good friends. So he started **The Civil Life Brewing Co.** with two of his closest friends, including head brewer Dylan Mosley. The Civil Life, housed in a rehabbed newspaper-distribution warehouse in Tower Grove South, has a simple philosophy, Hafner says: "Make great beer, and support the local restaurants, bars and community."

Jake Hafner

Kevin Lemp (no relation to St. Louis' historic Lemp Brewery) helped sell wine before venturing to make beer at **4 Hands Brewing Co.** He and brewmaster Will Johnston, a former Goose Island brewer who studied at Siebel, plan to incorporate some aspects of wine into the brews they'll make at their site about a half-mile south of Busch Stadium. Lemp and Johnston sourced used chardonnay and cabernet sauvignon barrels to fill with beer, letting the wood impart its nuanced flavors into the brews. "I want to make beers that evolve in your glass as they warm up, so that the last sip tastes different than the first one," Johnston says.

Is there room in the sandbox for everyone to play? The brewers say yes, and St. Louisans have proven that they will drink all the locally made beer they can get their hands on.

"There is always room for good beer," Johnston says. "The more brewers here, the more great beer we make, that just raises St. Louis' profile to the rest of the world."

Tom Schlafly

Tom Schlafly, whose St. Louis Brewery sparked the city's craft-beer revolution when it opened in 1991, agrees. He says he doesn't mind the competition, so long as it helps St. Louis remain synonymous with beer – great beer.

CRAFT BEER SAYS CAN-DO TO CANS

For most of its lifetime, canned beer has conjured images of the cheap swill that's found in Grandpa's fridge or crushed on the foreheads of frat boys.

But craft breweries are working hard to lift that stigma by putting their big, full-flavored beers in cans and hoping beer lovers put their bottles down and see the benefits of canned beer.

"Cans are really perfect vessels for beer, because they eliminate the chance of light or oxygen ruining it," says Brian Owens, brewmaster at O'Fallon Brewery, which in 2010 started canning its popular Wheach beer. "The trick is getting beer drinkers to realize that cans actually deliver a really good product."

There are other advantages, too. Breweries save money on shipping costs and labels, because cans weigh less than bottles and don't require labels to be printed and glued. Cans are made of more recycled material than bottles, making them environmentally friendly. And, canned beers can be enjoyed in places where glass is off-limits: float trips, sporting events, concerts, even airplanes. Virgin America sells beers from San Francisco's 21st Amendment Brewery on its flights – a first-class upgrade from most domestic light lagers available in-flight.

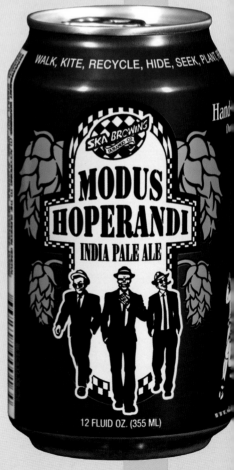

The first U.S. craft breweries to put a major focus on canning their beers – Oskar Blues in 2002 and Ska the next year – were in Colorado, where outdoor activities play a big role in beer marketing. Ska's cans, for example, have words like "float," "kite," "hike" and "fish" around the lip, encouraging people to enjoy their beers outside.

About 100 other craft breweries have discovered the allure of canning, and it seems like every day, another one is announcing plans to can. In St. Louis alone, craft-beer drinkers have more than a dozen options of different styles of canned beer – everything from easy-drinking lagers (Ska Mexican Logger) to hopped-up ales (Tallgrass Oasis).

BY EVAN S. BENN

Here are some of my favorite canned craft brews, all of which are available around St. Louis except for Oskar Blues and Southern Star – worth seeking out via trades or on your next trip where they're distributed.

Caldera IPA • I love this Oregon-made India pale ale for its deep orange-honey color and the way the sticky, piney hops jump out of the glass (like bottled beers, canned products should be poured into a glass for optimal aroma and flavor).

Big Sky Moose Drool • Don't let the name fool you – this beer tastes like neither moose nor drool. It's a brown ale with mild nutty and caramel flavors and 5.1 percent alcohol. It's hard to imagine a better session beer for a fishing trip.

New Belgium Fat Tire • For many drinkers, this amber ale was a gateway from macro to craft beers because it's flavorful, approachable and balanced. I did a side-by-side comparison of Fat Tire from a can and from a bottle, and I couldn't detect any difference in appearance or flavor.

Ska Modus Hoperandi • This year-round American-style India pale ale is not only one of the best canned beers out there, it's among the best beers in the country, period. I like to say drinking a Modus is like biting into a grapefruit – a citrus-rind snap followed by huge bitter-sweet hop juiciness.

Bottles up:
If you do choose to go with bottles, the best way to store them is upright, not on their side, which can cause oxidation and bad-tasting interaction with the bottlecap.

Oskar Blues Gordon • The writing on the can promises this double IPA will be "big, red, sticky," and it delivers. The brewery gets tons of well-deserved accolades for its Ten Fidy imperial stout, but I'm here to tell you that Gordon is just as impressive.

Southern Star Buried Hatchet Stout • This is a gem from a Texas brewery that makes only a handful of styles. With a huge coffee nose, caramel-chocolate flavor and creamy mouthfeel, it hides its 8.5 percent alcohol content extremely well.

'...AND DISTILLERY'?

Several St. Louis breweries have started to produce their own lines of artisanal spirits, which is why you'll see the words "and Distillery" tacked on to the names of places that many people associate primarily with beer. Like craft beer, the spirits that come from microdistilleries often are produced in small batches using high-quality ingredients.

Square One Brewery & Distillery became Missouri's first licensed microdistillery when it launched its Spirits of St. Louis line in 2008. The liquors include a whiskey made with cherrywood-smoked malt, a vodka distilled from locally sourced grains and a gin that is spiced with something Square One's brewers know plenty about: hops.

Amalgamated Brewing & Distilling Co., which runs the Stable brewpub in Benton Park, got into the distilling game in 2009. Its 85 Lashes Rum is made in copper stills from pure cane sugar and molasses, then aged in French oak barrels. Other popular small-batch releases from Amalgamated have included a grappa made with grape skins from Charleville Vineyard in Ste. Genevieve and a brandy made with peaches from Illinois' Calhoun County.

Crown Valley Brewing & Distilling Co. opened a state-of-the-art brewhouse in Ste. Genevieve in 2009 and quickly started adding distilling equipment, with plans to launch a full line of spirits. As of spring 2011, Crown's distillers were still testing batches of their first planned release: vodka.

BY EVAN S. BENN

Alex Ihnen and Michael Allen of St. Louis talk over beers at Amalgamated Brewing Co.'s the Stable in Benton Park, one of a few local breweries that have started producing distilled spirits on-site.

CHAPTER 11 # WHAT'S NEXT?

BEER GETS SOCIAL

As craft beer's popularity continues to grow and brewers continue to innovate, it's difficult to predict the next big trends with any degree of accuracy. Will sour be the new hoppy? Will Anheuser-Busch InBev gobble up as many small breweries until it becomes an even bigger force than it is today? It's hard to say. Here are some of my guesses as to where the industry is headed, and a few things of which I'm fairly certain:

GUESS

The pendulum will swing back toward **flavorful session beers.** We've seen it happen in the food world, where avant-garde cuisine or molecular gastronomy seemed to be replaced in recent years by simpler, more rustic dining options. Craft beer has always been about a focus on high-quality ingredients muddled as little as possible, and I think the trend toward extreme, highest-alcohol-ever, in-your-face beers will fade. What (I hope) will replace it is a move toward beers that have enough flavor to make you want another sip without having so much alcohol or bite that they assault your palate. A perfect example is **Half Crown,** a "session" IPA that's been on at Urban Chestnut since its first day in business. It has so much personality and oomph, I always have to check to make sure I haven't misread the chalkboard that says it's only 4 percent alcohol by volume.

The Boston Beer Co., maker of Samuel Adams, made a limited-release beer in 2010 with celeb chef David Burke that was brewed with grilled beef hearts. **Burke in a Bottle** is said to have a mineral, salty aftertaste from its bloody bizarre ingredient.

Scotland's BrewDog brewery raised the bar on extreme beer – and raised some eyebrows – when it released **The End of History** in 2010. The brew clocked in at 55 percent alcohol by volume (the strongest in the world, for about a week, until a Dutch brewer made a 60 percent ABV beer) and each of the 12 bottles produced came stuffed inside roadkill carcasses. The bottles quickly sold for $750 a pop.

CERTAIN

Social media is the new bikini marketing. True, it's hard to replace the persuasive power of a multimillion dollar ad campaign capped by a high-profile Super Bowl spot, but the fact remains: The most successful companies right now are the ones that have harnessed the power of social media. Does that mean that television beer commercials and billboards with girls in bikinis playing beach volleyball are going to go away? Fat chance. What it means is that the breweries that take the time to actually interact with and engage their customers on a one-on-one basis – the way that sites like Facebook, Twitter and YouTube allow them to do – are going to be the ones that build the most loyal, ardent supporters. And that – not ads with scantily clad models – is how you make your product stand out among dozens of others on beer-store shelves and at bars.

Mikkeller **Beer Geek Brunch Weasel** is one of those beers you could serve to friends, who would delight in how good it tastes, until you surprise them by telling them what's in it: coffee beans that have been eaten and excreted by Southeast Asian civet cats. If you can get past that, you'll see this Danish-made coffee stout is one of the best available.

CERTAIN

Mobile technology will change the way we purchase beer. You can read more in this chapter about how mobile apps are making us smarter, savvier beer consumers. But the power of smartphones to improve our beer-drinking experiences goes far beyond apps. Breweries have begun to roll out QR (quick-response) codes on beer packaging, allowing consumers to scan the product at the beer store and find out everything from its freshness to its ingredients and calorie content.

GUESS

St. Louis will become the next major craft-beer destination. Brewers are coming to St. Louis from Chicago, Denver, Minneapolis – big-time beer cities – because they see a potential here to become the Next Big Thing in the craft-beer world. And why not? We have the history. We have the drinkers. All we need is a few more restaurants, a few more bars and a few more certified Cicerones to really pride themselves on taking beer to the next level (and, ahem, maybe a few more direct flights in and out of Lambert), and St. Louis could easily find itself a travel destination for brew enthusiasts around the globe.

CERTAIN

Cans will be as common a beer vessel as bottles. The upsides to cans are virtually endless. Compared to glass bottles, they're cheaper to produce and less expensive to recycle, quicker to cool down, easier to transport and store, less prone to skunking from oxygen and light, more portable for places like beaches, golf courses, airplanes and concert venues, and the list goes on. The number of craft breweries putting their beers in cans more than doubled in 2010, and I don't see this trend curbing anytime soon. Craft beers will increasingly be packaged in cans – and that's perfectly fine with me. Let's just find a way to line cans with BPA-free materials.

CERTAIN

Breweries will continue to go green. The process of making beer is one that requires lots of water and energy. To help offset their carbon footprints, breweries have gone to great lengths to reduce their consumption and do their part to be environmentally friendly. Some leaders in this field include Anheuser-Busch InBev, which has drastically reduced its carbon-dioxide emissions and water usage in recent years; Sierra Nevada, which harnesses solar power and now grows its own organic hops and barley; and New Belgium, which has run its brewery on wind power since 1999 and donates a portion of its annual proceeds to Earth-conscious causes. These sort of moves will continue to gain traction in the brewing world, from the smallest breweries selling their spent grains to local farmers, to the biggest ones cutting their resource consumption.

THE HIP HOPS APP

The Post-Dispatch rolled out a Hip Hops mobile application that allows users to take me with them while grocery shopping, bar hopping and anywhere else they may need some beer know-how.

Available now – for free – at stltoday.com/beerapp (that link only works on smartphones), the app is your one-stop shop for just about everything you need to know about beer in St. Louis and beyond.

What you'll find: my reviews and star ratings for more than 200 beers, searchable by brewery or style; plus notes and beer lists from about 50 bars, restaurants, brewpubs and retail shops around St. Louis that put a special emphasis on beer.

Not quite sure what the difference is between a barleywine and a brown ale? You'll find quick definitions for more than a dozen beer styles, along with lists of those types of beers in our database and where you can find them locally.

With the touch of a button, you can call the place you're thinking about going, go to its website, see its Twitter feed or get directions on a map from wherever you are.

But wait, as they say, there's more. Lots more.

WANT THE FREE HIP HOPS APP?

Point your smartphone browser to http://stltoday.com/beerapp

Or read the QR code below.

The first screen you'll see is my Hip Hops blog, so you'll always have the latest beer news at your fingertips. One click from there and the app will display my most recent tweets.

This app is meant to be our guide to help lead you to good beer, so we've included a "Passport" feature that lets you store your own reviews and star ratings for the beers you try. Unlike apps that broadcast to others what you're drinking and where you're drinking it, Hip Hops will keep your notes private; they're yours and yours alone.

And, because this is a free, Web-based app and not under the control of the iTunes store, we can update it whenever we need to – such as when I've reviewed a new batch of beers, when bars and restaurants change their beer lists, or when you give us ideas for other cool improvements.

Here's how it works: From your smartphone, go to stltoday.com/beerapp. You'll get a pop-up reminder to mark the page on your home screen. Select "OK." IPhone users should then tap the arrow at the bottom of the screen, then select "Add to Home Screen." Now, you'll have the app's icon displayed on your screen for fast reference.

It's time consumers had a mobile tool to help sort the swill from the sublime and to keep them abreast of the latest happenings around town.

So next time you're at the beer shop or bar and can't decide what brew you want, take the Hip Hops app out of your pocket and ask me for a recommendation.

MORE ON THE HIP HOPS BEER APP

Excerpted from an interview I did with craftedsocialmedia.com:

Q: What was the inspiration to develop this app?

A: St. Louis has a storied history as a beer town, and the Post-Dispatch has always tried to give the industry the attention it deserves, both through our business coverage of companies like Anheuser-Busch and through more features-based reporting of the local beer scene. That's where I come in. For the past two years that I've been writing the paper's Hip Hops blog and column, St. Louis has really seen an explosion of craft beer, from established out-of-state breweries that have started to distribute here to hotly anticipated new breweries opening up.

We got a quick sense of how much demand there was for immediate and updated beer information through outlets such as my Twitter handle (@EvanBenn) and the Hip Hops Facebook page (http://facebook.com/hiphopspd). But we wanted to have a place to tie together all that information, and present it to people in a way that allowed them to access it wherever and whenever was convenient for them.

Q: Who is the target user?

A: St. Louis beer drinkers. It's definitely a St. Louis-centric app in that all of the 50 or so bars, restaurants and retail shops we highlight are in the metro area. So a lot of that, coupled with the mapping technology we have in place and the location-based stuff we're working on, is going to be most beneficial to a St. Louis user. That said, there is a ton of info that will be useful to anyone who likes beer or is interested in learning more. The beers I reviewed for the app are mostly all available in St. Louis, but you can also find many of them in California, New York, Colorado, Florida, etc. There is a style glossary that obviously has no geographic boundaries. And our "Passport" feature, which lets you rate and review the beers you drink, can be used by anyone. In short, I think our primary demographic is St. Louisans who like beer and feel comfortable getting information via smartphones, but beyond that, we designed the app to be helpful to anyone with an interest in beer, regardless of where they live.

Q: What's the benefit of the app?

A: The major benefit is being able to have a St. Louis beer guide available in your pocket at all times. At a grocery store or bar and need help deciding what to get? Pull out the app and compare the flavors (and calories and alcohol content) of the beers you're considering. Find something you really like and want to remember it for next time? Save your notes in the app's Passport feature for future reference. Going out and want to know what beers a particular bar or restaurant serves? The app will show you the place's beer list, get you there on a map and give you the options to call the establishment or see its website and Twitter feed. Is everyone talking about IPAs, but you don't really know the difference between an India pale ale and a regular pale ale? Take a spin through the app's beer-styles glossary to brush up on your knowledge. Want to know more about that rumored cask of Count Hopula (I made that up, but it probably exists) being tapped tonight? Check the app for my recent blog posts and tweets.

Q: What are you goals with this initiative?

A: Same as with my column, blog, Facebook posts and tweets, the goal of the Hip Hops app is just to give people another tool to help them connect with beer. People are as passionate about beer as they are about food, wine, sports – anything. So I see Hip Hops as a forum for people to have that dialogue while also absorbing whatever else they want, be it news, reviews or just making connections with others in this community. The app – I hope – provides all that, in one convenient, free little package. Our work is far from finished, we know that. We have a lot of cool features we're working on to make the app even more interactive and to iron out a few existing glitches. We'll be updating it frequently, with new beer reviews and other data. The hope is that by constantly adding content, we're also adding value to our users' experience.

Q: What opportunities do you see with respect to smartphone applications?

As far as I know, we're the first newspaper company to have made a beer app like this. I doubt we'll be the last. Mobile content is so important in our current media climate, and its reach keeps expanding every day. Beer-wise, a lot of successful apps have been popping up recently – Untappd is a great example, so often described as "Foursquare for beer" – but certainly not so many that I'd say the market is anywhere near saturated. The trick, I think, is finding a niche group who needs/wants your app. For Hip Hops, that's beer in St. Louis.

OTHER BEER APPS WORTH A LOOK

Hoptopia • Craft-beer blogger Lee Williams says he wanted to create this mobile version of his website as an "intuitive means of sharing my beer reviews with as many people as possible." He's working on a "pro" version that he says will have "real beer-geek appeal." The current version is free via iTunes and Android Market.

> **Pros:** Creative, colorful reviews. Users can search by beer name, style or brewery. Shaking the app generates a random review.
> **Cons:** Because the app covers mostly small-production brews, it'd be nice to have a beer locator or a list of distribution states.

Budweiser American Ale Finder • This location-based app helps you find the nearest bars, restaurants and retail shops that sell American Ale. Free via iTunes and BlackBerry App World.

> **Pros:** Tapping into GPS technology makes this app convenient and easy to use. Color-coded map pins show where the user is in relation to bars, restaurants and retailers.
> **Cons:** Can take an awfully long time to load, especially when not connected to WiFi. Would be more useful if it helped locate more than just one beer in Anheuser-Busch InBev's substantial lineup.

Schlafly Beer • Developed locally by Grey Swan Corp., the St. Louis Brewery's iPhone app features detailed descriptions of many of the 40-some beers it produces, as well as links to Schlafly's tweets and monthly newsletter. Free via iTunes.

> **Pros:** Menus of what's on tap at both Schlafly brewpub locations. Clean design. Good information on different beer styles.
> **Cons:** Events page and draft lists get stale when not updated.

Metosphere Beer! • This cool new app will keep getting better as more people use it. You can upload your own beer photos and reviews to compile your own review archive, or share them with the world to help enrich the mobile beer community. Free via iTunes and Android Market.

> **Pros:** A built-in tool keeps stats on your favorite styles and average review ratings. Easy to save and e-mail your reviews to friends.
> **Cons:** Search results are photo-heavy, which creates the need for a lot of scrolling and can slow down the app. Reviews need to be better organized.

7,800+ Beer Brands! • With its fairly comprehensive database of beers, searchable by name, style or at random, this app is a good resource for drinkers who want to have a lot of information at their fingertips. Free via iTunes and Android Market.

Pros: Tons of beers. Great details like suggested serving glasses, temperature and food pairings.

Cons: Lots of incomplete information (some beers have alcohol percentages listed; many do not). Bare-bones interface can get boring quickly.

Nirvino Beer Ratings Guide • The only app in this group that isn't free, the Beer Ratings Guide is worth the dough. It keeps track of the reviews you add and incorporates them into a sizable database. Available for $2.99 via iTunes.

Pros: Search allows you to enter food or flavors to find ideal beer pairings. Sort by ratings or price. Users can add beers to their "cellar" or "wish" lists.

Cons: The "Quick Pick" feature, which recommends highly rated beers at various supermarkets, is awesome – for users who live in California; many of the highlighted beers aren't available in Missouri.

ST. LOUIS BREWERIES ON TWITTER

- @2ndshiftbrewery
- @4HandsBrewery
- @AmalgamatedBrew
- @buffalobrewco
- @CSBSTL (Cathedral Square)
- @TheCivilLife
- @crownvalleybrew
- @fergusonbrewing
- @morgan_street
- @PerennialBeer
- @Schlafly
- @SixRowBrewCo
- @SquareOneBrews
- @urbanchestnut

Jina Patel savors a Piraat Belgian-style ale while Colin Harris polishes off a Hitachino Nest White Ale at the International Tap House in Soulard, which offers hundreds of beers, but none from the Anheuser-Busch InBev brewery that's located less than a mile away.

ENDIX A **RESOURCES**

BREWERY CONTACT & TOUR INFORMATION

Here the most recent contact information for St. Louis-area breweries and brewpubs. Tour details are provided where available. Even many places that don't advertise tours will be happy to show you their brewhouse if you call ahead to inquire or ask nicely when you're there.

Note: Places marked with an * are production breweries only and do not offer on-site beers for sale.

See a lot of brewery phone numbers that end in 2337? Check out your phone's keypad: Those digits translate to B-E-E-R.

2nd Shift Brewing Co.*
• 1401 Olive Road, New Haven
• 2ndshiftbrewing.com
• steve@2ndshiftbrewing.com
• @2ndshiftbrewery

4 Hands Brewing Co.
• 1220 South Eighth Street, St. Louis
• info@4handsbrewery.com
• 4handsbrewery.com
• facebook.com/4handsbrewingcompany
• @4HandsBrewery

Amalgamated Brewing & Distilling Co. (The Stable)
• 1821 Cherokee Street, Benton Park
• thestablestl.com
• 314-771-8500
• facebook.com/amalgamatedbrew
• @AmalgamatedBrew

Anheuser-Busch InBev*
• 12th and Lynch streets, St. Louis
• budweisertours.com/toursSTL.htm
• 314-577-2626
• facebook.com/Budweiser
• Free tours 10 a.m.-4 p.m. Monday-Saturday and 11:30 a.m.-4 p.m. Sunday from September through April; 9 a.m.-4 p.m. Monday-Saturday and 11:30 a.m.-4 p.m. Sunday in May; and 9 a.m.-5 p.m. Monday-Saturday and 11:30-5 p.m. Sunday from June through August.

Augusta Brewing Co.
• 5521 Water Street, Augusta
• augustabrewing.com
• jeri@augustabrewing.com
• 646-482-2337
• Brewing takes place in Labadie; no tours.

Buffalo Brewing Co.
• 3100 Olive Street, St. Louis
• buffalobrewingstl.com
• feedback@buffalobrewingstl.com
• 314-534-2337
• @buffalobrewco

Cathedral Square Brewery*
• 3914 Lindell Boulevard, St. Louis
• cathedralsquarebrewery.com
• brewmaster@cathedralsquarebrewery.com
• 314-803-3605
• @CSBSTL

Charleville Vineyard Winery & Microbrewery
• 16937 Boyd Road, Ste. Genevieve
• charlevillevineyard.com
• info@charlevillevineyard.com
• 573-756-4537

The Civil Life Brewing Co.
• 3714 Holt Avenue, Tower Grove South
• thecivillifebrewingcompany.com
• @TheCivilLife

Crown Valley Brewing & Distilling Co.
• 13326 State Road R, Ste. Genevieve
• 573-756-9700
• crownvalleybrewery.com
• facebook.com/crownvalleybrewing
•@crownvalleybrew
• Thirty-minute tours are available
for $3 during regular hours.

Exit Six Pub & Brewery
• 5055 Highway N, Cottleville
• 314-282-5673
• facebook.com/exitsix

Ferguson Brewing Co.
• 418 South Florissant Road, Ferguson
• fergusonbrewing.com
• @fergusonbrewing
• 314-521-2220
• facebook.com/fergusonbrewingco

Highlands Brewing Co.
• 105 East Jefferson Avenue, Kirkwood
• highlandsbrewing.com
• info@highlandsbrewing.com
• 314-966-2739
• facebook.com/highlandsbrewing

Jacobsmeyer's Tavern
• 2401 Edwards Street, Granite City
• 618-876-8219

Morgan Street Brewery & Restaurant
• 721 North Second Street, St. Louis
• morganstreetbrewery.com
• 314-231-9970
• facebook.com/morganstreetbrewery
• @morgan_street

O'Fallon Brewery*
• 26 West Industrial Drive, O'Fallon, Mo.
• ofallonbrewery.com
• info@ofallonbrewery.com
• 636-474-2337
• Free tours by appointment,
generally 2 p.m. Saturday.

Perennial Artisan Ales
• 8125 Michigan Avenue, South Carondelet
• perennialbeer.com
• brewer@perennialbeer.com
• @PerennialBeer

Schlafly Bottleworks
• 7260 Southwest Avenue, Maplewood
• schlafly.com
• tours@schlafly.com
• 314-241-2337
• facebook.com/schlafly.beer.fans
• @Schlafly
• Free tours noon-5 p.m. Friday-Sunday.

Schlafly Tap Room
• 2100 Locust Street, St. Louis
• schlafly.com
• 314-241-2337
• facebook.com/schlafly.beer.fans
• @Schlafly

Six Row Brewing Co.
• 3690 Forest Park Avenue, St. Louis
• sixrowbrewco.com
• evanhiatt@sixrowbrewco.com
• 314-531-5600
• @SixRowBrewCo

Square One Brewery & Distillery
• 1727 Park Avenue, Lafayette Square
• squareonebrewery.com
• info@squareonebrewery.com
• 314-231-2537
• @SquareOneBrews

Tin Mill Brewing Co.
• 114 Gutenberg Street, Hermann
• tinmillbrewery.com
• info@tinmillbrewery.com
• 573-486-2275
• Self-guided tours daily; call for private
tours.

Trailhead Brewing Co.
• 921 South Riverside Drive, St. Charles
• trailheadbrewing.com
• 636-946-2739

Urban Chestnut Brewing Co.
• 3229 Washington Boulevard, St. Louis
• urbanchestnut.com
• info@urbanchestnut.com
• 314-222-0143
• @urbanchestnut

QUICK BEER STYLE GLOSSARY

Amber Ale (or Red Ale) • These medium-bodied, amber-hued beers typically display toasted-malt and caramel flavors and restrained hop bitterness.
  Examples: Budweiser American Ale, Charleville Tornado Alley Amber Ale, New Belgium Fat Tire.

American Lager (including Light Lager) • Mostly pale-yellow in color and clear with relatively low alcohol content or hop flavor, these easy-drinking lagers are sometimes brewed with adjunct grains like corn and rice.
  Examples: Busch, Bud Light, Sam Adams Light.

Barleywine (or Old Ale) • Stronger than many styles, barleywines will hit you over the head with their generous additions of hops and malts. The result is often a chewy mouthfeel that brings flavors of bracing hops and booze-soaked fruit.
  Examples: Sierra Nevada Bigfoot, Stone Old Guardian, Bell's Third Coast.

Brown Ale • This traditional English style tends to have translucent brown colors and a flavor profile of malty toffee sweetness and nuttiness.
  Examples: Big Sky Moose Drool, Avery Ellie's Brown, Ferguson Pecan Brown Ale.

Extra Special Bitter • Don't let the name fool you: ESBs really aren't that bitter at all. They're actually quite balanced, usually with bready, toasted-malt characteristics and a rich copper color.
  Examples: Ska ESB, Schlafly ESB Winter Ale, Deschutes Bachelor ESB.

Flavored/Spiced Beer • A catch-all style for beers with dominant flavors achieved through spices and other additions such as pumpkin, spruce tips, hot peppers, ginger root and more.
  Examples: O'Fallon Pumpkin Beer, Twisted Pine Billy's Chilies, Left Hand Good Juju.

India Pale Ale • Hops are the name of the game when it comes to this historic beer style. IPAs can taste and smell like citrus rinds, pine resin, tropical fruits or fresh-cut grass, depending on the varieties of hops used in the brew. Sub-categories include high-alcohol double or imperial IPAs, and American-style IPAs, which are typically feature American-grown hops.
  Examples: Bell's Two-Hearted Ale, Boulevard Single-Wide IPA, Stone IPA.

Oktoberfest (or Märzen) • These German-style lagers were traditionally brewed in March (märzen) and served several months later during the Oktoberfest celebration. The style typically produces beer with deep golden color and bready or toasted-malt flavors.
  Examples: Ayinger Oktober Fest-Marzen, Boulevard Bob's '47 Oktoberfest, Schlafly Oktoberfest.

BY EVAN S. BENN

Pale Ale • This ale style is what helped kickstart the American craft-beer revolution. They are similar in appearance to amber ales, but with a more aggressive hop profile. American pale ales favor mostly American hops, while versions with English hops often fall into the ESB category.

Examples: Sierra Nevada Pale Ale, Bear Republic XP Pale Ale, Schlafly APA.

Pilsner • This traditional lager style is light-bodied with low bitterness but an assertive aroma, usually from European-grown noble hop varieties that impart grassy, spicy or floral elements.

Examples: Morgan Street Golden Pilsner, Boulevard Pilsner, Samuel Adams Noble Pils.

Porter • A nice introduction to "dark" beers, porters can display flavors of dark chocolate and coffee from dark-roasted malts, but they shouldn't be extremely heavy or high in alcohol.

Examples: Six Row Strong Porter, Founders Porter, Urban Chestnut Harwood Myth.

Saison • These farmhouse-style ales that originated in Belgian and French countrysides have seen a surge in popularity among American craft brewers. Complex flavor profiles are led by yeast strains that express a fruity tartness and dry finish.

Examples: Boulevard Tank 7, Goose Island Sofie, Jolly Pumpkin Bam Biere.

Style surplus:
The Beer Judge Certification Program recognizes more than 125 categories and subcategories of beer.

Stout • Sort of like porter's big brother, stouts can range in color from dark brown to pitch black and contain a hefty mouthfeel. Subcategories include milk stouts, brewed with sweet lactose sugar; double or "Russian imperial" stouts, which have elevated alcohol contents; traditional Irish-style dry stouts; and flavored stouts with added coffee or chocolate.

Examples: Founders Breakfast Stout, Schlafly Coffee Stout, Left Hand Milk Stout.

Wheat Ale • This category includes German-style hefeweizens or weissbiers, which are unfiltered and brewed with yeast that produces aromas of banana, cloves or even bubblegum; Belgian-style witbiers, which are spiced with orange peels and coriander; and American-style wheat ales, which tend to let their crisp wheat flavors stand out.

Examples: Urban Chestnut Schnickelfritz (German), Cathedral Square Belgian-Style White Ale (Belgian), Bell's Oberon (American).

For in-depth style categories and descriptions, see the Beer Judge Certification Program's guidelines at bjcp.org.

BOOKS AND OTHER REFERENCES

Listed below are most of the works that aided me in my research and reporting for this book, as well as others that I've found particularly useful in my search for beer knowledge. – EB

Buchanan, Jean and Rose, Bob, editors. **Anheuser-Busch: The King's Reign. The History of the Brewery in St. Louis.** Marceline, Mo.: Walsworth Publishing Co. and St. Louis Post-Dispatch Books, 2008.

Hieronymus, Stan. **Brew Like a Monk: Trappist, Abbey, and Strong Belgian Ales and How to Brew Them.** Boulder, Colo.: Brewers Publications, 2005.

Herbst, Henry; Kious, Kevin; and Roussin, Don. **St. Louis Brews: 200 Years of Brewing in St. Louis, 1809-2009.** St. Louis: Reedy Press, 2009.

Jackson, Michael. **Michael Jackson's Beer Companion.** Philadelphia: Running Press, 1993.

Jackson, Michael. **The New World Guide to Beer.** Philadelphia: Running Press, 1998.

Oliver, Garrett. **The Brewmaster's Table: Discovering the Pleasures of Real Beer with Real Food.** New York: HarperCollins Publishers Inc., 2003.

MacIntosh, Julie. **Dethroning the King: The Hostile Takeover of Anheuser-Busch, an American Icon.** Hoboken, N.J.: John Wiley & Sons Inc., 2011.

Mosher, Randy. **Tasting Beer: An Insider's Guide to the World's Greatest Drink.** North Adams, Mass.: Storey Publishing, 2009.

Rother, Charlotte, and Rother, Hubert. **Lost Caves of St. Louis: A History of the City's Forgotten Caves.** St. Louis: Virginia Publishing Co., 2004.

Schlafly, Tom. **A New Religion in Mecca: Memoir of a Renegade Brewery in St. Louis.** St. Louis: Virginia Publishing Co., 2006.

Bethany Davis grabs beers from a refrigerator at the International Tap House in Soulard, which stocks its bottled beers according to country, and state, of origin.

ACKNOWLEDGEMENTS

Like the Daily Miracle that we know as the newspaper, this book was result of a collaborative effort that involved far more people than possible to name. But please allow me to mention a few.

Wade Wilson is an enormously talented and patient colleague whose experience in conceptualizing and designing previous Post-Dispatch books proved invaluable not only in getting this project out, but in making it look good.

Photography Director Larry Coyne, Features Photo Editor Hillary Levin and photographer Johnny Andrews – along with Wade – coordinated, shot and edited most of the artwork in this book.

Mike Smith, P-D online sports editor, and Jody Mitori, features editor (and my direct boss) handled the editing – a thankless job that they performed admirably and without complaint. Jody deserves an extra mention for filling in on many of my day-to-day duties while I was out of the office writing.

Bob Rose, the P-D's deputy managing editor of presentation and a fan of beer, has been instrumental in delivering our beer coverage to readers across multiple platforms, from our app to this book. Publisher Kevin Mowbray and Editor Arnie Robbins also have been supportive of this work, and I'm grateful. And our partners from the Sales & Marketing team, Angie Clark and Cory Parolin, also deserve thanks.

My sources, friends, readers and everyone else in the St. Louis beer community – especially the passionate drinkers from STL Hops – are an absolute pleasure to interact with every day. I've found brewers and brewery owners here to be unfailingly generous with their time and knowledge. And if such a thing as a beer snob exists, I haven't run into him or her yet. The enthusiasm St. Louisans have for beer is infectious, never obnoxious. Listening to people talk about their love for beer, and getting to share their stories, is an experience I hope to treasure for many years to come.

Last, and most important, my family deserves recognition for being a constant source of encouragement and support, in this endeavor and all that I set out to pursue. Mom and Dad, thank you for being understanding on the deadline nights when I was too stressed to talk on the phone. And Teri, my love, your work ethic is an inspiration to me, and your neverending kindness and warmth remind me every day how lucky I am.

ABOUT THE AUTHOR

Evan S. Benn covers the beer scene for the St. Louis Post-Dispatch.

His Hip Hops column, blog, mobile app and social-media pages can be accessed at stltoday.com/hiphops.

Benn is an award-winning journalist who grew up in Pennsylvania (drinking Yuengling Lager), graduated from Northwestern University's Medill School of Journalism in Chicago (Goose Island 312) and worked as a Metro reporter at The Miami Herald in Florida (mojitos) before joining the Post-Dispatch in 2009.

The Riverfront Times named Benn Best Newspaper Columnist in 2010, and in 2011 Metromix/KSDK ranked him among St. Louis' Top 10 Twitter users (@ EvanBenn).

Benn lives with his wife, Teri, in downtown St. Louis.

Detail of bicycle rack formed in the shape of a beer mug outside of the Ferguson Brewing Co. in Ferguson.

PHOTO CREDITS

POST-DISPATCH PHOTOGRAPHERS

Johnny Andrews • 27, 40, 44, 47, 70, 72, 73, 74, 75, 85, 86, 88, 89, 90, 92, 94, 95, 96, 98, 99, 100, 102, 104, 111, 114, 116, 126, 127, 128, 130, 132, 134, 140, 159

Evan S. Benn • 79, 81

David Carson • 31, 82

Robert Cohen • 22, 23

Stephanie S. Cordle • 12

Wayne Crosslin • 21

Karen Elshout • 56

J.B. Forbes • 38

Elle Gardner • 24, 76, 78, 151, 157

Christian Gooden • 28, 29, 107, 108, 120

Erik M. Lunsford • 20, 22, 33, 36, 80, 123, 124

Huy Richard Mach • 19, 106

Dawn Majors • 10, 30, 66, 67, 83

Kevin Manning • 15, 43, 68

Jerry Naunheim Jr. • 32, 77, 103

Post-Dispatch files • 9, 13, 14, 15, 16, 23, 46, 138

Laurie Skrivan • 42, 79, 82, 83

Jason E. Taylor • 110

Tom Uhlenbrock • 50

Larry Williams • 39

Adam Wisneski • 40, 112

OTHER PHOTOGRAPHERS

Katherine Bish • 118, 119

Sarah Conard • 71

Sid Hastings • 48

Diane L. Wilson • 17, 51, 52, 53, 54, 56, 57, 58, 59